DRAWING ON
EXPERIENCE
IN ADULT
AND CONTINUING
EDUCATION

DRAWING ON EXPERIENCE IN ADULT AND CONTINUING EDUCATION

Paul Jay Edelson, Ph.D.
Dean of the School of Professional Development
Stony Brook University

KRIEGER PUBLISING COMPANY
MALABAR, FLORIDA
2006

Original Edition 2006

Printed and Published by
KRIEGER PUBLISHING COMPANY
KRIEGER DRIVE
MALABAR, FLORIDA 32950

Library of Congress Cataloging-in-Publication Data

Edelson, Paul Jay.
    Drawing on experience in adult and continuing education / Paul
    Jay Edelson.
        p. cm.
    Includes bibliographical references and index.
    ISBN 1-57524-248-6 (alk. paper)
        1. Adult education—United States. 2. Continuing education—
    United States. I. Title.

    LC5251.E34   2006
    374'.973—dc22
                                                    2005044484

    10   9   8   7   6   5   4   3   2

CONTENTS

PREFACE

A career only makes sense retrospectively. While you are busy living it, there are more important things to worry about than how you got where you are. What now appears inevitable was often problematic at best, with plenty of doubt and confusion along the way.

Like almost all of my colleagues, I fell into continuing education and found that I liked it, that it resonated with me in very personal and fundamental ways. Certainly there are easier and less stressful paths to making a living in higher education. Just take a look at your own campus. I suppose it is this very challenge of succeeding that has held the strongest attraction for me. That's why I've persevered for over 30 years.

Continuing education is always a test. You can never take accomplishment for granted since something is bound to change, upsetting whatever equilibrium you may have temporarily achieved. The pot is always bubbling, ready to boil over. Fortunately there is more than one way to achieve one's ends. Otherwise I would not have prevailed, since my way has not always been the easiest or smoothest, in fact, quite the opposite. Resilience, flexibility, and a commitment to core values are a few of things that have gotten me through the toughest times. Good colleagues too, even though I'm frequently going against the grain of established practice, ruffling the feathers of even my closest friends.

I've tried to write this book as a series of conversations that might take place after hours at a conference, when friends are kicking back, exchanging stories and anecdotes about what it's really like being a dean or director of continuing education. I envision a group of us talking into the night. We have diverse backgrounds and experiences, and come from different parts of the country, from big schools and small, some of us are young and some aren't, all united by our common dedication to adult learning.

So sit down and pull up a comfortable chair. We're just getting started and there is much to talk about and share.

ACKNOWLEDGMENTS

I never could have predicted my career in continuing education. Ups and downs, successes and disappointments, the only consistency has been the unwavering support of my wife, Leta. Her encouragement has kept me going, even when I was ready to give up. Our children, Shari and Avi, have also hold a special place in my progress. After all, being a parent is without question the most significant form of continuing education.

A word of thanks to my colleagues Von Pittman and Joe Donaldson who have always shared my enthusiasm for the scholarship of adult education and who gave valued input throughout the process of writing this book. To those who reviewed early drafts: Kay Kohl, Michael Shinagel, Ron Cervero, Jim Novak, Wayne Ishikawa, Maureen Connolly, Tom Kowalik, Stephen Schneider, and Eric Streiff, I appreciate your candor and perspicacity.

A special note of gratitude is owed my editor Mary Roberts at Krieger Publishing who matched my enthusiasm and contributed her wholehearted support to the project. It was Mary who suggested the title *Drawing on Experience*. Elaine Rudd also edited the manuscript and mightily contributed to its readability.

Throughout the book I identify others who have helped me in my journey. To all of you, and countless others, I am so pleased that we could work together and that I had the good sense to profit from your experience and advice.

THE AUTHOR

Paul Jay Edelson has served as Dean of the School of Professional Development at Stony Brook University since 1986. Hr edited *Rethinking Leadership in Adult and Continuing Education* (1992) and *Enhancing Creativity in Adult Education* (1999 with coeditor Patricia Malone). Other works include *Weiterbildung in den USA* (2000), *The Complete Book of Distance Learning Schools* (2001) with Jerry Ice, and the monograph *Higher Education's Role in Retraining Displaced Professionals (1997)* with Jane O'Brien and Marlene Brennan which received Best Publication of the Year Award (1998) from the American Association for Engineering Education. He has also authored over one hundred presentations and papers on diverse aspects of adult learning. He is the recipient of the Research and Scholarship Award (2003) of the University Continuing Education Association.

As a Visiting Guest Scholar, Edelson has lectured at Aristotle University (Thessaloniki), University of Messina, University of Florence, SCO-Kohnstamm Institute for Educational Research at the University of Amsterdam, Indira Gandhi National Open University/IGNOU (New Delhi), the Autonomous National University of Mexico/UNAM (Mexico City), the German National Institute for Adult Education/ DIE (Bonn), and at the University of Lapland in Rovaniemi, Finland.

Edelson attended Brooklyn College (BA, 1966), the University of Minnesota, and New York University (MA, 1970, Ph.D., 1973). His other interests include painting, studying foreign languages, and riding horses.

INTRODUCTION

I started thinking seriously about this book in March 2003 when I was honored with the Research and Scholarship Award of the University Continuing Education Association (UCEA) at its annual conference in Chicago. Here I was, being recognized by my peers for all my papers, articles, books, and presentations. Each one added to the one before, eventually yielding a massive body of work. I was suddenly reminded of something I had read decades earlier in Richard Armour's *Going Around in Academic Circles, A Low View of Higher Education* (1965). Armour's imagery was of a scholar building a pile of writings so high that he could stand on top of it and "pluck a full professorship" (p. 122). Brilliant little cartoons accompanied his text.

I read Armour's book when I was a student in New York University's (NYU) Higher Education Program studying for my Ph.D. and preparing myself for what I hoped would be a successful career in higher education administration. This was in the early 1970s which, you may recall, was a very contentious time in American life, characterized by opposition to the war in Viet Nam, campus unrest, militant civil rights advocacy, all within a general ambiance of what was then called the "counterculture." Why I thought I would succeed in higher education now eludes me. In fact, I had just been fired from my first academic job, as assistant to the Director of Administrative Services at NYU. It's all very strange when I look back.

Maybe the humor and practical advice found in Armour's book and also in Norman Runnion's *Up the Ivy Ladder, The Delicate Art of Climbing in the Academic World* (1969) gave me the confidence that I too could ultimately prevail, if I followed the steps outlined in these slender books. What's more, they made campus life sound like fun, filled with smart people who, when they were not reading, writing, or traveling, liked to intrigue against each other. This was also the theme in Francis Cornford's *Microcosmographia Academica, Being a Guide for the Young Academic Politician* (1969, 1908), the granddaddy of collegiate self-help books. Written by a savvy and cynical Cambridge don, the book has invaluable suggestions, such as recommending when to walk around campus in order to "casually" bump into your collegial quarry. By the time I read Cornford I had landed my own deanship and was desperately searching for the helpful advice and critical skills needed to survive.

I'm not too proud to admit it. I was in over my head in my early days at Stony Brook University, as my story will later make clear. I called friends at other universities, but their advice was generally too abstract and general ("make friends with the faculty") to be of any use. The literature too was a disappointment, dwelling on the esoteric world of marketing and program development with the notable exception of Malcolm Knowles *The Making of an Adult Educator* (1989). But this book, written by a seminal figure in adult education, though inspirational, was more about the overall field of continuing education, with very little to say about higher education.

I blundered along until it finally started to make sense, through trial and error, countless meetings, and numerous intense conversations with other deans and directors. I've made my share of errors and been thrown out of more than one office, even thrown a punch or two myself. Yet, I've succeeded. Beyond the scholarship, I'm even more proud of my accomplishments as an administrator and educator. Now, in the spirit of Cornford, Armour, and Runnion, I wish to offer some helpful guidance to my fellow continuing education practitioners, both young and old, and especially to those new to the field. I know there are others with more years under their belt, working in larger institutions, with more impressive resumes. Still, I'm willing to bet that the journey I describe in this book will resonate with your own personal experiences, even if it is only your first year on the job!

Rather than a journal or a more conventional narrative, here is a collection of observations and analyses of the world of continuing higher education from the perspective of a dean whose field of action is principally that of part-time adult students.

There is no real chronology other than I began my first continuing education job in 1972 and now it is 2006. Although I have moved around and held positions in various settings, I still do similar things, albeit the institutional context and office technologies are different. But not the students. Regardless of program type or academic level, they come to be improved, changed, and prepared for a better life through education, and it is my job is to help them. It is also my job to generate resources for my institution in the form of enrollments and revenue. How to simultaneously balance these two goals is also an important part of this story.

I've taken the liberty of including some of my sketches, hence the word "drawing" in the title. I'm hoping that these too contribute to a helpful and enjoyable read.

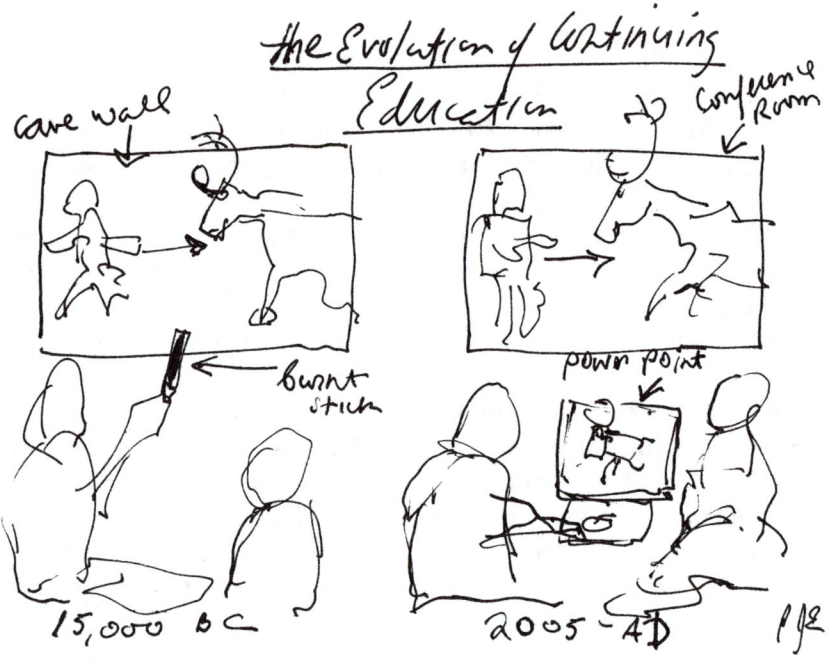

CHAPTER 1

An Introduction to Continuing Higher Education

Images of Continuing Education

Hothouse Blooms

I was once told by a campus electrician at my first collegiate job at NYU that higher education was everything above the basement. Well, continuing education is everything that is left over, after all the other campus deans and administrators have carved up the pie. This includes all the things that no one else wants to worry about or do: night school, noncredit courses, different types of community outreach, usually the summer session, programs with industry, labor unions, the bypassed and under and un-employed. It is a strange amalgam of the programs that don't fit in anywhere else, the loose ends, or a quick response to short-term needs that strangely enough often become a long-term commitment, stretching way beyond the horizon.

If you are new, and looking for a way of understanding our field, be assured that continuing education at each college is a "hothouse bloom" very much suited to the conditions of that particular school with very little luck of being successfully transplanted in its original form to another campus or college. Unlike traditional academic disciplines, no one type of continuing education is normative. One school, because of where it is located, may have extensive executive training programs while another, with a more rural location, might specialize in distance learning degree programs that are addressed to a statewide clientele. Still other schools could have extensive worldwide programs, and others recruit students no farther away than a subway ride.

This lack of standardization also extends to size, running the gamut from a single director at a small college with one half-time assistant, to deans at enormous universities, public or private, with staffs of hundreds, not counting part-time faculty, which can add many more hundreds to the total. The variations between programs are too numerous to list, but I can assure you, there is not a single campus continuing education unit or division that is a mirror image of another. Surprisingly, differentiation also extends to sister colleges within a single state university.

When I first came to Stony Brook in 1986, I had little more than the foggiest notion of what a Dean of Continuing Education was supposed to do. I decided to call my counterparts at the three other State University of New York university centers. At the University at Albany my position did not exist, although there was a very large state government training operation, led by the director at Albany's Rockefeller Institute. At the University of Buffalo, the Dean of Millard Fillmore College ran the undergraduate night school. There were also four assistant deans in charge of continuing education for their respective professional schools. At Binghamton University, continuing education was at that time a component of the School of Education, with the dean wearing two hats. My program at Stony Brook was a horse of a different color, a separate graduate degree granting unit of the university, without a faculty, that also conducted noncredit programs.

In the course of my career I learned that there is nothing surprising about the varieties of continuing education projects, programs, methodologies, and modes of organization. This is not strange if you bear in mind the essential elements common to all programs, namely the linkage of continued learning with achieving greater success and satisfaction in life. With that as its core, continuing education can veer in a multitude of directions, incorporating all sorts of self-improvement offerings, degree and non-degree curricula, different types of learning experiences from the most casual to the most formal and minutely prescribed, and presented to all types of students. This instrumental role and relationship to individual growth is so obvious in our culture, we shouldn't be surprised that more applications keep cropping up as further needs are continuously identified.

One of the glorious features of the continuing education world, from the perspective of practitioners, is the mind-boggling variety of things to do. If you think about it, everyone is a potential student. And without a doubt, everyone you meet has had some contact with the wide-ranging world of adult learning—dance lessons, computer courses, workplace training, conferences, workshops, you name it. This universal frame of reference makes it hard, if not impossible, to say "no" whenever a new need or idea emerges. In short, if you are not versatile, flexible, and open-minded, this field is not for you.

Cash Cows

Burton Clark, grappling with the rather jumbled nature of adult education programs, used the term *omnibus* as a way of describing a number of different program components all nestled together within the same organizational container (1980). Each continuing education activity represented another passenger on the bus, all traveling in a common direction. Years ago I tried to come up with unconventional ways of viewing continuing education (Edelson, 1991). Part of my motivation was to provide alternatives to the all-pervasive marketing model that emphasizes revenue to the exclusion of other factors, the so-called *cash cow* wherein viability is an outcome of registration-generated income or related quantitative measure. Successful programs, or cash cows, are milked to keep the continuing education enterprise afloat. Experienced managers learn how to anticipate the life cycle of programs and when the cash cow will eventually run dry. New programs must be sufficiently developed to maintain constant productivity.

This marketing model, appropriated from the business world, is so pervasive in continuing education that it is of-

ten uncritically accepted a priori and frames definitions of
a program's success or failure and that of individual careers.
Operationally, the model determines which audiences will
be served and the types of educational activities that can
be offered. Strategic planning in this sales-oriented environment becomes very similar to product development in
the business world. Positioning, market research, course
development, advertising, and promotion become significant administrative activities. Course evaluations are
viewed as ways of measuring consumer satisfaction and
identifying new course ideas.

Without doubt this corporate-inspired model, stressing
the development of marketable programs, has been able to
successfully address the need for identifying high demand
programs, assuring acceptable levels of quality, and, most
importantly, satisfying the financial requirements imposed
upon continuing education by the institution. Its uncritical
acceptance, however, has dampened enthusiasm for experimentation with other approaches to program development
and continuing education administration that might equally
suffice under current conditions. Moreover, while it may
not be feasible, or even desirable to jettison this marketing
model, creative professionals may find ways to modify it,
thereby mitigating its most noxious aspects.

A Variety of Images

Being able to visualize different models for continuing
education becomes a key element in thinking of alternative
organizational approaches. In fact, it is the most meaningful type of strategic planning since it is fundamental and a
prelude to the development of programs and their implementation. Standing back from the marketing model and
viewing it as one of many possible realities, we can become
architects of our personal visions for continuing education
that come closer to reconciling professional needs with institutional requirements.

Here are my 12 additional ways of conceptualizing our
field. In reality these are images or metaphors rather than

fleshed-out models. Nevertheless, it is interesting to see how examples from biology, politics, organizational theory, and everyday life can contribute to our understanding and, hopefully, our virtuosity as professionals.

1. **Amoeba**. Having no fixed shape or form, this model is opportunistic and fluid. It can move in many different directions simultaneously, taking advantage of the environment. An example is organizing contract training with business and industry when this is in demand, and at the same time offering teacher training for local school districts. It will allocate resources on an as-needed basis, without a fixed, permanent commitment to any single function.

2. **Third World Country**. Within the geopolitical world of the university, continuing education is an underdeveloped, exploited, and poorly capitalized region producing students and generating income for very little investment. The dean's job could be understood as securing political and economic autonomy so that continuing education can chart its own destiny, casting off its colonial status and achieving true independence, equality, and statehood.

3. **Laminate**. Lamination fuses or joins a number of different structural components producing a new substance that can be extremely strong and durable. A continuing education laminate might include a number of well-defined functions, such as contract training, conferences, and short courses that are performed both efficiently and effectively. All elements have an important part to play; the laminate is internally egalitarian by definition.

4. **Ghetto**. Like the Third World metaphor, the ghetto is shaped by political forces. It is a place to segregate marginal populations. There is also a paucity of resources allocated to serve them. Part-time students

are a peripheral clientele for many colleges and universities. By fixing this responsibility within a defined school or division, service can be provided, at least to a minimal degree.

5. **Sailboat**. The sailboat is moved by the wind, first one way and then another. Like the amoeba image, it must take advantage of shifts in the environment or changes in the market. Unless it has auxiliary power, it can be stranded far from shore. The sailboat drifts or moves without ideology or belief system. It is shaped by the natural forces of its environment, taking advantage of the program opportunities that exist, going with current and breeze.

6. **Mélange** or **Mixture**. The ingredients comprising continuing education consist of many different programs, blended into a flavorful mélange or stew, perhaps like a delicious *bouillabaisse*. The chef, or dean, needs both expertise and good taste to ensure a satisfactory outcome. Making a delicious and wholesome meal from unusual ingredients strikes me as a good description of what I am often able to do. On the negative side, its improvised nature means that today's product may not the same as tomorrow's or the following day's.

7. **Research and Development (R &D) Unit**. Continuing education, with its open structure and receptiveness to the market, becomes an excellent location to try new programs and launch innovations. Some of the features of higher education we now take for granted (summer school, professional education, women's studies, off-campus, and outreach) had their origins in continuing education units. For those who love to experiment, viewing continuing education as an educational laboratory is useful imagery. Online education is a current example of how a new technology can be quickly exploited by those in exten-

sion and continuing studies, and then subsequently exported to other campus bureaus.

8. **Settlement House**. Like Jane Addams's Hull House in Chicago, continuing education may be seen as a means of reforming and improving society. It is a type of educational settlement house where the bypassed, disadvantaged, and newly arrived can be prepared for reentry into the society, retooled for competition and hopefully success. Continuing educators belong to a helping profession in the classic sense of health care and the clergy.

9. **Radical Movement**. For those dissatisfied with the conservative accommodationist settlement house, continuing education can be a way to directly engage and refute mainstream values. To be successful requires a passionate commitment to the ideas of equality, access, opportunity, and political freedom. Think of a community storefront, not an ivy-covered campus. For the radical it is all about adult education as a utopian mission to recast society and its basic ideologies.

10. **Mediator**. Colleges are often viewed as complex, highly abstract bundles of critically important esoteric research and scholarly activity which are impossible to grasp by outsiders, either discretely or in their totality. Continuing education as an "applied" area takes research and reconstitutes into something more readily understood and appreciated by laypersons. This model, then, places continuing education at the interface of the larger, external community. In spirit it is similar to the image of the front porch coined by Joe Donaldson. This is where town and gown can meet and learn about each other in a relaxed, friendly manner. On the front porch, trust is nurtured, leading to future productive collaborations and relationships.

11. **Facilitator**. A popular image, continuing education as facilitation supports other university programs. This may include scheduling, enrolling students, budgeting, providing logistical support such as classrooms and media, and conducting evaluations. The unit may even develop the program concept and then take it to an academic department which supplies a faculty member for instruction. Benign and symbiotic, the facilitator performs a unique and specialized role. Critics, however, find it subordinated and reactive, and a convenient target when programs do poorly.

12. **Bureaucratic Process Management**. This model suppresses the content of continuing education in favor of administrative procedures. This could include enrollment management, similar to what transpires within the realm of a college admissions office or providing the administrative coordination of the summer session. It is a restricted vision that downplays the creation of new programmatic initiatives.

In summary, the 12 metaphors illustrate several distinguishing features of continuing education that obtain in all (or just about all) of its variants. They are market-driven, outward-looking, student-centered, experimental, and relatively egalitarian and reform oriented, run in a business-like manner, by people who see themselves as pragmatic, yet idealistic, problem-solvers whose roles are not easily subsumed under the existing categories of faculty or administration. Students are more likely to be part-time, or if they are full-time, it is for a very short periods. By whatever criteria used—age, occupation, or marital status—they qualify as adult, the role of student being just one facet of fast-paced, multilayered lives. And as mentioned earlier, they view education as an instrumental goal essential to achieving other important objectives. If not education for its own sake, this is certainly education for the sake of a better life personally, professionally, and as members of a community.

Metaphor-making is an enjoyable pastime. But it must be acknowledged that all attempts at simplifying continuing education fall short of the baffling complexity that actually exists. A model that may successfully describe what we are today simply cannot predict what action or direction will be or should be taken in the future. Moreover, beyond adding function after function, we also require an overarching value structure or ideology, an internal guidance system that is rock-steady, regardless of the shifts of wind or institutional priority du jour. Each of us needs, as a foundation, to determine why we selected a career in continuing education from among a multitude of other avenues and directions. Otherwise we surely will be blown, like the sailboat, one way and then another.

I hold a vision of a better world made possible by lifelong learning. I believe that by incrementally improving access and opportunity for individual advancement, we are making a positive difference in our society. This has been my compass, pointing to a true north, regardless of job position or place of employment.

"Wanted: Utopian Idealists, Willing to Work for Long Hours and Earn Less than Others. Preferably Able to Derive Great Satisfaction from Small, Incremental Accomplishments."

The above is a take-off on an early advertisement for Pony Express Riders in the American West (Di Certo, 2002, p. 44): "Wanted—Young Skinny, Wiry Fellows Not Over Eighteen. Must Be Expert Riders, Willing to Risk Death Daily. Orphans Preferred." In both examples, what might be potential deficits in other ways of earning a living are proclaimed as desirable and positive, if not mandatory.

Go to any gathering of continuing education professionals and it will quickly become apparent that you are among an idealistic, hardy, optimistic, and resourceful breed, accustomed to but not intimidated by adversity. Although I am a city boy by birth, and for a good part of my life, I am tempted to see our hardy band as farmers. We are aware of the many potential problems that can and will precede a harvest, yet like clockwork, we are out working in the fields from dawn until dusk. Maybe this is another manifestation of my weakness for descriptive metaphors, but I think it sheds light on the single-minded dedication and faith that are customarily found among our colleagues. If there are lazy continuing educators out there, I have yet to meet them. I remember going to conferences where the workshops began early in the morning and didn't conclude until way after the sun set. And we were all away from our offices, with no one watching or to impress.

Some may argue that this devotion to activity substitutes for intellect and intelligence, in effect the brawn, not the brains, of the collegiate enterprise. By this perspective we are the laborers who shovel the coal in the boiler room while the more talented and enlightened, high up on the bridge, chart a course for higher education, as suggested by Kett (1994). Similarly, the fiscal accountability and discipline of continuing education managers are viewed as merely offsetting the lack of productivity and inefficiencies that run rampant on every campus. "If only continuing education would make more money" is a recurring refrain in every university budget office. Fortunately we are "profitable" enough in a world of spendthrifts and profligates to be viewed as successful capitalists, even if the label doesn't accurately match the cloth.

From my perspective, continuing educators are the true heirs of the Enlightenment, embodying the democratic and egalitarian ethos that higher education today is elsewhere sorely lacking. Where else will you find a belief in the liberating effects of knowledge or a universal concern for student learning and accomplishment? A sensitivity to multifaceted adult lives? A dedication to providing value? A comprehension of the fundamental linkage of educational opportunity with economic and political freedom? And a commitment to the bypassed, disenfranchised, and exploited? Continuing educators seek to level the playing field so that those who have been previously discouraged and dissuaded from pursuing their education can now do so with greater ease.

Coming to Continuing Education

The roots of my own interest in continuing education began at Brooklyn College where I was an undergraduate from 1962-1966. "BC" (as we called it, provincially unaware of the other BC up in Boston) opened my eyes and mind to the limitless opportunities of higher education and learning. Although I didn't realize at the time, the liberal arts curriculum would become a metaphor for my life and my diverse educational enthusiasms. As a freshman, a course on ancient history stimulated a very brief desire to become an archeologist. Then another course where I learned about the scourge of the sea lamprey in the Great Lakes nudged me towards marine biology. This seesawing from one field to another occurred on a regular basis, in fact in direct response to the many interesting courses in which I enrolled. I just couldn't decide where to put my intellectual marbles! I ended up with a major in history but also with concentrations in comparative literature, art history, and political science.

I took more courses than needed to graduate...my desire to learn was, and still is, apparently insatiable. Truth be told, my grades were not of the highest. In retrospect I attribute this not so much to the competitiveness of my school, but more to my uneven intellectual skills. Although I would study hard and long, high grades seemed to elude me. Still, I was undeterred by the prospect of yet another C. I graduated knowing a little about a lot which is still my leitmotif.

This was all in the midst of the burgeoning civil rights and antiwar period, freedom rides and sit-ins, when students made the transition from Marlboros to marijuana and from sleepovers to sleep-ins. An interesting manifesto of this period is *The Strawberry Statement* (1969), a memoir of the Columbia University student revolt written by participant James Kunen. Naturally, it seemed, I threw in my lot with the agitators, protestors, civil rights advocates, and rebels. Luckily, I eventually found a career, which at that time I never knew existed, where this meandering, challenging pattern, which some university colleagues see as an intellectual and thus moral flaw, could be considered a strength, if not a preferred characteristic.

My graduate studies were initially at the University of Minnesota in American studies, an interdisciplinary program where many fields came into play including economics, folklore, history, literature, sociology and the arts. Still, at the time (1966-1968), what I perceived as the isolation and irrelevance of scholarship from the major events of our generation grew into a source of disillusionment with the entire academic establishment. I subsequently tuned in, and turned on and dropped out, to paraphrase LSD guru Timothy Leary. Years later, when I entered, purely by accident, the world of continuing education, I was overjoyed to find a beachhead from which to assault the mainstream. And fortunately for me, universities have traditionally made space for those challenging the status quo. But usually the status quo that is being confronted is not that of the university itself. When this happens the university can behave just like any other conservative establishment.

At times continuing education can be seen as a type of equal opportunity bureau within elite research universities, serving as a bridge for those less traditionally prepared, whose lives are less convergent with scholarship, and whose goals do not usually incorporate long-term scientific discovery or academic achievement. These part-time adult students are here to earn a promotion, raise, or licensure, or to earn degrees and certificates that will help them qualify for the next rung on their occupational ladder. From time to time I have heard faculty refer to these mundane "meat and potato" objectives as less valid compared with those of students seeking entry to the academic professions, itself merely another form of vocational education. The goals are the same; they are only assuming different forms.

Within this framework, our jobs as continuing educators become making our students' paths the most direct, the least cluttered by obstacles, and the shortest possible in pursuit of their goals. We seek to offer convenience in scheduling and administration, generous course selection, high quality, rigorous instruction that is at the same time attuned to the constraints of adult life, and a range of degrees, certificates, and credentials that are relevant to the aspirations of our clientele.

The fast-paced life of continuing education, especially in program development, attracted me from the outset. Perhaps, its concreteness, the palpable connection between hard work in the here-and-now and the ability to see the outcomes of my efforts, I found immediately appealing. I remember once while I was a graduate student at the University of Minnesota conducting research in the library stacks. These were seemingly suspended from the roof of the library building, along the outside walls of the structure, and appeared to float on narrow steel wires— somewhat like the Brooklyn Bridge with its too-taut cables.

I had a study carrel, actually no more than a wire cage with a shelf for books and a 40-watt bulb overhead nestled amongst the millions of volumes that are the holdings of a typical major American research university. I was studying the history of child labor in the United States. Feeling just about incarcerated and overwhelmed by the tons of materials surrounding me, I felt in a truly visceral way that academic life, especially the self-imposed solitude of scholarship, was not for me.

Perhaps I was more influenced by the "cracker barrel" ambiance of my father's hardware store in Gerritsen Beach, Brooklyn. This was an out-of-the-way location nestled against the south shore of Jamaica Bay. His business, The Mart Store, was your prototypical small hardware store. It contained innumerable uncountable items, some of whose purpose was no longer apparent. It is one of life's ironies

that my dad, who lived in an apartment house and never
had to lift a finger or repair anything, could invariably recommend the right tool or part for whatever obscure job his
customers were tackling.

His special expertise was based upon knowing, not necessarily doing. This, in a strange way, is a fitting hallmark
for my life in continuing education where I developed programs on hearing aid dispensing, Bach, dental and medical
technology, Haydn, Degas, and the extermination of termites
— sometimes, I must admit, with only the scantiest knowledge of pesticides or fugal form. It would be a mistake, however, to assume that my lack of hands-on knowledge dis-
tanced me from the demanding realities of program development in these and other subjects.

I'll Quit When It Stops Being Fun

One of my favorite *New Yorker* cartoons by Mike Twohy
shows an ant straining under the weight of a huge stone it
is carrying uphill. Along the way, it quips to a lady bug loung-
ing nearby, "I'll quit when it stops being fun." This illus-
trates the near workaholic ethos of continuing educators I
mentioned earlier. While others are off campus between
semesters, and also during the summer, enjoying the south
of France or some other exotic locale, we are at our desks
pounding out the work, developing new programs and the
like. I've often wondered if we in continuing education are,
in fact, the ants of the university world, toiling on the
ground, while the tenured faculty soar way above us like
eagles?

If not stoking coal in the boiler room of higher education, another unflattering view of our field places us among
the ranks of campus auxiliary services along with the bookstore, dining services, security, and parking. Is continuing
education just another support function? Of course this is
not even remotely true despite the superficial resemblance.
Our role is distinctly different. We educate a large group of
students whose needs would not otherwise be met. Con-

tinuing educators believe wholeheartedly in the concepts of extension and outreach, and in helping people better themselves through education. We also love the dynamic, volatile world of adult learning, where today's solutions won't necessarily work tomorrow.

Many of us now holding leadership positions came up through the ranks of program development. This is the journeyman role wherein we learned to assess market demand, identify faculty resources, develop programs, and then launch and evaluate them. At the time we entered the field, there were few graduate programs in adult education, so we learned by doing. We rarely have the time or resources to do things by the book, including the use of needs assessments. Instead, we fly by the seat of our pants, mostly by instinct, based on experiences both good and bad. This is one of the few professions where if you are able and willing to try again, you can. The life of the continuing educator is one of constant improvisation. Do you like working without a detailed script, inventing as you go along? Do you welcome the challenge of each year trying to do better, in terms of students, programs, and revenue? Can your ego withstand the ongoing abrasion of sarcasm from those who don't ascribe to our values? If the answers are "yes, yes, yes," please read on. This may be the field for you.

Lessons Learned

We work in a complex field where no two university or college continuing education programs are alike. If you require a template that tells you what to do, you won't find it. You'll attend numerous conferences with your peers and listen to their great ideas and successful programs only to be disappointed when you find that they don't seem to work when you try them at home. There are many ways to approach adult education. You don't have to be limited by your current institution's value system. Try to stake out a position where yours and theirs converge.

CHAPTER 2

Community College Continuing Education

My first professional contact with adult education was at New York City Community College (NYCCC), also called City Tech, in downtown Brooklyn, where I was initially hired as the Evening Administrator. I took this part-time job while I was a doctoral student in the Department of Higher Education at New York University's School of Education. Little did I know I was embarking on what would prove to be a lifelong career. Incidentally, my matriculation in the Higher Education Doctoral Program followed frustrating, intense periods of short-term jobs including working for a shirt company in the Empire State Building, being a secondary school substitute teacher, and being an administrative assistant at NYU. I had finally come to the realization that I wanted to return to higher education in some capacity, but didn't know where or how. I also realized I didn't want to be anyone else's assistant.

I learned about NYU's Higher Education Program while I was taking summer courses to obtain my teaching license. The department's office was right next to that of the Social Studies Department, so in a sense I moved right down the hall, after a brief and unsatisfying stint of junior high school teaching. The NYU doctoral program trained college and university administrators. Almost all of my fellow students already had jobs; I was an exception. The typical matriculants were middle-aged, mid-level, middle-class males working in colleges located in either New Jersey or on Long Island. They could be in admissions, finance, or some other administrative area including adult education. Without a doctorate their mobility was limited, and they knew it. So they trudged into class after work and then slumped home.

Back in the era prior to e-learning we part-time evening students had no other alternative to commuting by train, car, or bus. A good number never finished, and remained in the higher education no-man's land of the ABD (All But Dissertation). Luckily I had a research fellowship in the department, and could initially devote my full energies to earning the doctorate. But after a year the meager stipend was no longer adequate for my needs as a newlywed. A fellow NYU student told me about a vacancy at City Tech where he had just been hired. The Director of Extension was looking for an additional part-timer, but one who could work weekdays from 12:30 pm-8:30 pm, and on Saturday mornings until noon. She was also a student in the NYU program completing work on her degree. I had finished all of my course work by this time and was also writing my dissertation, so the odd hours did not present a problem, except that of being out-of-phase with my City Tech colleagues. Even in continuing education, this feature of being out-of-step with others has distinguished me throughout my career.

In the Division of Continuing Education and Extension I was the person who was on duty after everyone else on the staff had gone home. Mine was the one light at the end of a long dark hallway. Students came in to drop off checks, argue about late fees and closed classes, or just look for information. For faculty I photocopied papers and exams, distributed rosters, called their spouses, and occasionally put dimes in the parking meters.

The job was an odd assortment of things that had to be done, but which no one else found time for during the day. It was a miniworld of loose ends, within a school of apples and oranges, mismatched parts and beliefs. My duties were principally in the sector of fee-supported courses. Other staff members did literacy programs in prisons, grant-funded programs for the disadvantaged or physically challenged, or joint projects with labor unions. With the exception of a handful of people like me who were on the Ph.D.

track, the other young professionals in the division were coming at continuing education from the field of social work and had Master of Social Work degrees. This perspective dominated and there was a good deal of talk about social radicalism and reform. I wonder if this is still the case in community college continuing education? My job however, had a different, more practical, literally down-to-earth trajectory.

Pest Control Operations

New York City, then and now, and most likely into the future, besides having one of the densest human populations in the world, also has an animal population to match. In this case I'm talking about the zillions of roaches, bugs, rats, feral cats and dogs, pigeons, starlings, everything disagreeable in the animal kingdom that people want to rid themselves of. Without exaggeration, public health issues alone make this a most serious challenge. Add damage to property and the degradation of public and private life, and you have a major problem that simply can't be ignored. You also have a billion-dollar business devoted to the eradication and extermination of pests. This can't be accomplished without the assistance of carefully trained and licensed personnel. Understandably this became one of the community college's most popular and well-enrolled programs.

Pest extermination is a dirty and disagreeable job that relies upon a workforce made up of new immigrants, with partial knowledge of English, and little formal education. It is not hard to conjure up the serious implications of powerful and lethal chemicals in the wrong hands. The college acted as a certifying and licensing agency for the city and state. Our job was to make sure that the students graduating from our courses would scrupulously use pesticides, baits, and traps according to the very rigid criteria established by manufacturers and the Department of Health. Since in exterminating, training tended to be on the job,

our classes contributed a formal dimension addressing subjects that could not be taken for granted or overlooked. Passing the course meant that you would receive your professional license and could be hired as an exterminator. Thus
a failure meant the loss of a job, actual or potential. Very
serious consequences indeed. Our instructors were the senior entomologists and pest control specialists for the New
York Department of Health, so criteria for passing were
demanding yet fair.

One night while I was on duty, a student accompanied
by an older friend appeared at my desk. After some initial
discussion it became clear that he had twice failed the pest
control course. He obviously did not think that taking it
again would improve his chances and had devised another
direct, but highly illegal, approach to his goal, namely brib-
ery. The student's friend removed from his pocket a wad of
greenbacks and offered these to me in return for a passing
grade. I was momentarily stunned, and then, with warning
bells going off in my head, vigorously rejected the offer. In
hindsight, with the benefit of much experience, I am now
not as shocked as I was then. Today's students, instead of
bribes, are more likely to use the threat of legal action or
the leverage of a political connection to get their ways. The
student whose money I quickly rejected was operating
within the rules of his own milieu and was also probably
advised that "this is how it is done."

The incident vividly brought home to me the connection
between education and the ability to earn a decent income.
Today, at Stony Brook University, I deal with students studying to become classroom teachers, school superintendents,
engineers, or managers. The stakes are the same even
though the salaries are much, much higher. My students
now are better educated and have higher standards of living, but they are still motivated by the desire to improve
themselves, for reasons of personal accomplishment or for
what it will mean for their families. That evening at City
Tech I learned in a unique way that continuing education is
a serious business.

The Varieties of Urban Continuing Education

The course "Pest Control Operations" was followed by other related courses I developed including (naturally) "Advanced Pest Control Operations" and "Termites, Carpenter Ants, and other Wood-Damaging Organisms." I sat at the apex of a broad pest-control pyramid with hundreds of students enrolled each term. Of comparable popularity was "Driving Instructors Education" which prepared students for licensure by the N.Y. State Department of Motor Vehicles as a certified driving school instructor. In a totally different vein, "Preparing the Cold Buffet" was taught by a professional chef in the college's own well-equipped teaching kitchens. In this course aspiring caterers learned the nuances of delicately carving a radish rosette, preparing an ice sculpture in the shape of an eagle with outstretched wings, or delicately coating a foie gras in aspic. Other students learned how to purchase large quantities of meat, test someone's hearing, or fit a pair of glasses in our courses in, respectively, "Bulk Food Purchasing," "Hearing Aid Dispensing," and "Ophthalmic Dispensing."

Each course provided a view into a different occupational and social world, with its own standards and even aesthetics. For example, Herb Barath, who taught "Preparing the Cold Buffet," was a famous New York chef. At his suggestion I attended a major exposition held in the old Coliseum on Columbus Circle that was a sort of world series of the culinary arts. The top chefs of all the private clubs (Yale, Harvard, New York Athletic Club, etc.) and the restaurant world all tried to outdo one another with tour de force artistic creations. Magnificent ice sculptures and buffet displays worthy of the Metropolitan Museum of Art vied for the judges' attention. I never knew that these kinds of things existed. For myself, I was inspired to learn how to carve a radish, to slice and dice, and to pay attention to the artistry of cuisine. I can also whip up a neat egg cream, but not because of NYCCC. My friend's father owned a luncheonette in Brooklyn and I worked there after high school classes.

A Temporary Setback

Program development of noncredit, fee-supported courses was my prime responsibility at City Tech. This is the traditional backbone, the bread and butter of continuing higher education. Almost all universities offer these short courses, so-called because they usually run for less than a semester. Some schools, notably those in densely populated urban areas, run what are called program shops with course offerings numbering well into the hundreds each term. Successful programs can generate in aggregate millions of dollars in revenue, but it is safe to say that most continuing education offices are more modest and attempt to cover their expenses and to perhaps generate a little extra for the campus. Hence, the search for a successful, well-attended course is an ongoing quest for the continuing educator's holy grail, regardless of institutional type or location.

Here I am in 1972, a newly minted member of the extension team. Suddenly I had an identity. I could go to a party of adults and say I developed outreach courses for a living. It was at one of these gatherings that I met someone who worked on Wall Street and who pitched me an idea for a program that would make "tons of money." I heard the siren's call of the ringing cash register and for a period lost my self-control, if not my sense of reason. The course he proposed would train people to sell stocks and securities, a field I knew nothing about then and the same is lamentably true now. We developed mailing lists of hundreds of New York metropolitan area brokerage firms where we were "sure" to find scores of potential students. We printed fliers, labeled and stuffed boxes and boxes of envelopes. It was very labor intensive work in those days. And yes, you guessed it, not a single student for our efforts! But interestingly, I learned a valuable lesson: just move on to the next program....as quickly as possible! But a small scar remained. It almost prevented me from achieving success with a real continuing education blockbuster at the Smithsonian.

Failures

A few words, first, about "failure" in continuing education. In our culture so much is written about success that it
is tempting to minimize its opposite as a brief, temporary
bump in the road. Would that this be true. Unfortunately,
failure is as much a part of an adult educator's life as frequent strikeouts were to the legendary Babe Ruth. And I'm
talking about embarrassing strikeouts, like the one I just
described.

It's almost inevitable that these will occur, since we are
so often trying to identify a new program area and get there
before other competitors. And we are working at breakneck
speed, multitasking every inch of the way. I've had so many
flops—at City Tech, the Smithsonian, and at Stony Brook
University. Sticking with the baseball metaphor, you've just
got to wait for your next at bat and hope that you will do
better. If you are easily embarrassed by what others will
regard as flagrant acts of apparent ineptitude, please re-
consider, for your own good, this particular vocation. Remember this, the flops keep coming, even after 30 years;
but only if you are doing the job right. If you play it safe by
just offering iterations of popular courses (Pest Control I,
II, III) in the way that Hollywood will keep producing se-
quels to popular movies, there will quickly come a time when
this strategy dead-ends, and even you have to plow new
programmatic fields.

Some of you who have had the benefit of adult education graduate programs will say that the use of rigorously
developed needs assessments will mitigate program can-
cellations. Let me caution you. Data is always incomplete;
we see what we want to see; respondents tell us what they
think we want to hear; we never have enough time or the
resources to properly conduct this research; and on and on.
Time for a confession: I've never done a needs assessment.
Never. And yet at the Smithsonian, as I will relate in the
next chapter, I churned out money-making, well-enrolled
courses one after the other, year 'round, for 10 years. There's

a simple rule that all good continuing educators know and I will share it with you later. Yet, be advised, I still bombed on a regular basis. Obviously, to survive like the Bambino, you have to have more than your share of home runs. But the strikeouts are the price you pay for swinging for the fences.

Conflicts and Tensions

At City Tech I learned that night school was a big business with thousands of dollars in earnings hanging on the outcome of a single course. And where wanting to make a better, more equal society through enhancing educational opportunity was not an unusual goal for a young person to have, although achieving it was another issue entirely. For me, there clearly was, and continues to be, an omnipresent tension between institutional standards of success and what I wished to accomplish. Was a young course coordinator to be judged by earnings at the turnstile or by amount of progress toward achieving an amorphous ideal of equality and opportunity? It is clearly easier to assess the former than the latter. Moreover, achieving one set of goals could very well be at the expense of the other. That is, if success is measured by chasing markets of students with the ability to pay, what about those who cannot?

This is a problem that is raised in every continuing education textbook, and provokes much argument between "theorists" and "practitioners." Do "markets" drive out "causes"? Is there a perverse Gresham's Law of Adult Education where your very success takes you further away from your ultimate goals? I began to ruminate on these conflicts while at the same time thinking about further expanding my pest control and tungsten inert gas (TIG) welding night school empire.

I also saw and experienced for the first time another continuing education paradox, that being the disconnect of continuing education from other bureaus of the college. This was not so much in course work, but in ideology and values.

You might think that the practical goals of continuing education would be perfectly in tune with the down-to-earth, career-oriented community college. But, you would be wrong. I am not just commenting on City Tech, but on community colleges in general, based upon decades of conversation with my continuing education colleagues working in that sector. Does simply labeling an area of endeavor "continuing education" make it suspect in the eyes of other academicians regardless of institutional type? Or is it the credit/noncredit divide? It couldn't be "night school" since much of any community college's offerings take place in the evening. The same is true with serving older students since junior colleges are close to being true intergenerational communities. This is less so at traditional colleges and universities where the 18-24 age cohort still predominates (60%), but by less and less each year. Not surprisingly, at the graduate level 80% of the students are 25 and above; in truth it is just about all adult education (Aslanian, 2001, p. 4).

Dyer's *Ivory Towers in the Marketplace* (1956) offers us a clue. This was the first book-length treatment of the evening college phenomenon in the United States. Written in the postwar heyday of economic prosperity and seemingly boundless college expansion, Dyer is uniquely attuned to the urban night school, its sudden rise of popularity, the skepticism of day college faculty and their charges of "soft pedagogy" and low intellectual quality (p. 17). The prejudice against night school, he maintains, is falsely based on exaggeration, anecdote, and the prior negative experiences of some day school faculty who occasionally taught at night. For a more contemporary example, see the article "A Little Night Teaching" (Morse, 1986).

At the crux of their belief is the erroneous assumption that if the night school students and faculty were any good, they would be attending or teaching full-time during the day. Sadly, this thinking still prevails. Do not be surprised to discover the presumption of diminished commitment, divided loyalties, half-hearted application, and a less than standard skill-set among the students you serve and the faculty that teach them. Fortunately, as more full-time faculty and campus administrators learn about this population, the more their appreciation of it grows. Lately there has also been a fiscal incentive to value this population. Nevertheless, we have reached a stage in our culture where part-time learning is so common, especially at the graduate level, even becoming an expected part of the adult experience, that the false stereotype of inferiority finds less and less traction with each passing year.

I found the world of continuing education at City Tech to be a godsend; especially after the other false starts I had in trying to find a career. My newly discovered organizational talents coupled with a natural intellectual curiosity enabled me to move from one task to another, addressing bureaucratic paperwork as well as the ongoing need for new course development. I frankly enjoyed the variety in my work, the exposure to so many different areas of learning, and the unusual mixture of the people teaching in these programs.

In my four years at NYCCC in addition to fee-supported courses, I also administered a Vocational Education Act funded grant to help hearing impaired adults learn office skills. This too was a completely different world with its own language (American Sign Language), culture, and complexities. My schedule shifted from night to day, and I began to see more of my colleagues and the diversity of our bureau. It was a three-ring circus of experimentation and pilot programs. Dean Victor Lauter was our head, but Associate Dean Fannie Eisenstein was the heart of the operation, with her commitment to social change through education.

It was during this period that I determined to become a Dean of Continuing Education, a wish realized 14 years later at Stony Brook. I would have stayed at City Tech for the remainder of my career, but deep budget cuts by the City of New York in the mid 1970s jeopardized my grant-funded position and I began searching for something new and hopefully more stable. Answering an ad in *The New York Times* I soon found myself pulling up stakes and heading for Washington, D.C, and the Smithsonian Institution. It was a dramatic shift from the gritty world of downtown Brooklyn. But, as the French say, "the more things change, the more they stay the same."

Lessons Learned

Learn from your mistakes. You've got to make them in order to grow. Being a continuing educator means that some people, perhaps in your own institution, will question your career choice. Ignore them since they, or others like them, will always be there. Make the most of where you work and explore all the opportunities. Although I was at City Tech for only four years, these were filled with meaning. By addressing the needs of historically marginalized populations I felt that I was contributing to the betterment of society. Yes, at times, I was compromised by the requirement of revenue generation, but not entirely. The community college outreach agenda serves a critical adult education mission and I was fortunate to have played a contributing role.

CHAPTER 3
At the Smithsonian

The Nation's Greatest Theme Park

My first impressions of the Smithsonian Institution (SI) took place just before Independence Day in 1976. I was there for my job interview which fortuitously coincided with this unique celebration of our country's 200th birthday. Patriotic bunting, thousands of tourists, Air Force jets streaking overhead in formation; everywhere was a feeling of festivity and happiness. The interview was scheduled for the ornate, hundred-year-old Arts and Industries (A&I) building situated right next to the Smithsonian Castle, itself an architectural icon of the first order. I remember entering the A&I building after passing through the Smithsonian's Victorian Garden. This was a sumptuous treat for the senses, especially sight and smell. There were follies and frills galore. It even featured banana trees bearing fruit. You can only imagine the contrast with New York City Community College, the prototypical stark urban campus of concrete and steel, with a handful of scrawny trees struggling to survive.

I had to traverse the A&I building and saw on display thousands of artifacts from the 1876 Philadelphia Centennial Exhibition including operating steam engines, patent models of all sorts, weaponry, and a huge statue of Gambrinus, the Flemish king who allegedly discovered beer. He was straddling a keg, hoisting a beer mug in welcome of my arrival! In the director's office there were antiques galore. And we spent the first part of my interview talking about art. Elegance was everywhere: the setting, the glitz,

owls in Tower here

Famous Building known all over world!

Smithsonian Castle From Garden

A cool place to have lunch

and glamour, the full extent of which I couldn't even conjure. And the beautifully dressed men and women; did places
like this actually exist? How could I be so lucky to have this

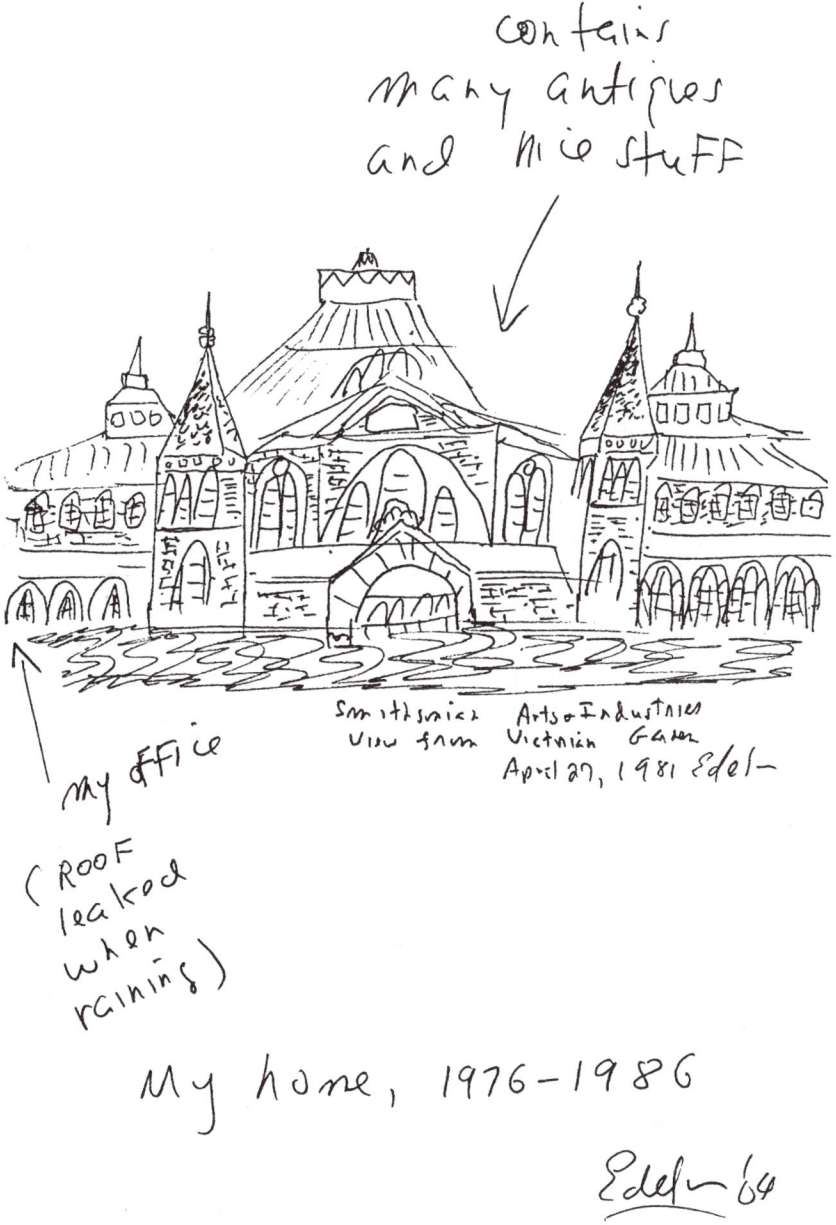

contains
many antiques
and nice stuff

Smithsonian Arts & Industries
View from Victorian Garden
April 27, 1981 Edel—

my office

(ROOF
leaked
when
raining)

My home, 1976-1986

Edel— 64

opportunity? I returned home star-struck and reluctantly resumed my City Tech schedule as if nothing had happened. When the magic phone call offering me the job suddenly came, I couldn't believe my good fortune and accepted immediately, without much haggling, even though we would have to relocate so that I could start in just a few weeks.

Decision-Making Styles

I've always envied those people who are somehow able to take their time and carefully weigh the merits of every offer. They calculate, bargain, and then calculate some more. At Stony Brook University I have seen this strange dance between employer and would-be employee stretch out over a semester, sometimes longer. I don't do that. Instead I have always jumped at each new opportunity and made a quick deal, with a minimal amount of back and forth haggling. Yes, I do land the job, but am I sacrificing a better deal? Of course I will never know since real life is not exactly a laboratory. But it is something to consider.

Simerly and Prisk (1992) have written an essay on the art of negotiating employment contracts written specifically for directors of continuing education. Perhaps they too had made some hasty decisions? I wish I could tell you that I was able thereafter to successfully follow this advice in my career. But that is getting ahead of my story for now. I will just state that the "quick deal," for better or worse, has been the hallmark of my career. The real upside is that this way I get to make a lot of decisions, and evidently more have been right than wrong. In essence, this is my style. You can only imagine how I have gotten along with the more phlegmatic types I have known, including administrative superiors. Let me put it like this, the tortoise cannot run with the hare, or better yet, the hare cannot crawl with the tortoise. Ever. If forced, it is a most painful experience for both. At a dedication of Stony Brook's Workforce Development Center, one of our state senators praised me for my alacrity, which in his case meant getting in to see him, getting the money for this new enterprise, and then getting out without taking too much of his time.

Unlike several others I've worked with, I've never suffered from "analysis paralysis." But am I, on the other hand, too impulsive? It depends what side of the fence you are on, and on your own decision-making style. The main thing is that you've got to determine this aspect of your administrative character (see Skinner, 1999). As a consequence of my own impetuosity, I have tended to hire more deliberate staff members to give me that essential sounding board. Sometimes there are fireworks when senior staff vociferously disagree with each other and with me. But it's worth the price for sound decision making. I pride myself, however, on making up my own mind, following both my insight and instinct. Interestingly, I've found that after making a rather fast decision, I typically engage in profound soul-searching and second-guessing. I justify this behavior by reminding myself that I was able to make a difficult decision without letting too much doubt get in the way.

My New Job

The Smithsonian was everything City Tech was not. Black tie instead of blue collar. A worldwide reputation, a blue chip among blue chips. Beyond the complex of museums in Washington, later augmented by the Cooper-Hewitt in Manhattan, there are extensive research stations all over the world where Smithsonian scientists conduct their fieldwork. In cooperation with Harvard University, the Smithsonian operated the Smithsonian Astrophysical Observatory. And then there is the National Zoo and the Air and Space Museum, as well as a score of other projects and institutes, *Smithsonian*, a well-written and attractive magazine, with beautiful photos. I was joining one of the most visible, complex, and far-flung cultural institutions in the world. No more pest control or welding. But still the same continuing education bottom line of cold cash.

My position was Director of Courses for the Smithsonian Resident Associate Program (RAP). This was a self-supporting bureau of the Smithsonian that was expected to generate revenue for the institution through its courses, events, trips, and workshops. In effect, it was the Smithsonian's continuing education division. The course division was responsible for four 8 week terms that corresponded to the seasons. My unit generated about 100 courses per term, and we were always programming. I likened myself to a hamster in a cage— running round and round. RAP was example of a continuing education program shop. Customarily these are located in large universities where the surrounding population density makes for a large potential audience. Therefore, it is not surprising that our institutional models and benchmarks were New York University, the New School for Social Research, and the University of California, Berkeley, all outstanding examples of continuing education that had, in fact, elevated the noncredit course to an art form.

Our audience was composed of the many well-educated people drawn to Washington who were usually employed in some aspect of government work, such as the military and the many civil service offices that proliferated in downtown D.C., spreading out into the suburbs. Overall it was a very cosmopolitan group; almost all had at least a bachelor's degree and a surprising number had either lived or worked abroad, or were members of the large diplomatic community living in the District. Pleasing this group was not always easy. And because it was *the* Smithsonian, with its illustrious reputation, there was little margin for failure. Our programs were often based upon the Smithsonian collections and research activities and drew upon SI curators and also the broader range of first class expertise in the greater D.C. area. In addition to the universities, this could include speakers from the Brookings Institution, the National Geographic Society, the Organization of American States, and so forth.

There was so much new information about the Smithsonian that I had to master, I found myself working well into the evenings and on weekends just visiting its museums and galleries. This exercise taught me a valuable lesson on the importance of cutting back extra hours to the strictly essential. There were plenty of times when I had to stay late including the first week of classes for each of our terms. Logging in more hours than absolutely necessary over time sapped my strength and diminished my ability to concentrate and be mentally sharp during the day. Of course each person has to know when and where to draw the line. Now if I think someone on my staff is putting in too many hours, I say, "Cut back and don't worry about it." The work will always be there in the morning. Why wear yourself out? It's not a sprint, but a marathon.

Cash Cow, Gift Horse, Golden Goose

The Smithsonian's continuing education program was a real cash cow; it generated millions of dollars annually. In addition to courses, RAP sponsored individual lectures by high-profile notables like Carl Sagan, I. M. Pei, and the Dalai Lama; children's programs; art and craft courses; and trips and tours. At that time it was one of the most comprehensive liberal arts, noncredit adult education enterprises in the country.

Being housed on the Washington Mall, between the George Washington Monument and Capitol Hill gave us a nonpareil location. Just saying to prospective speakers that you were calling from the Smithsonian mitigated the reality of our paltry honorarium which was a flat, all-inclusive fee of $300 for out-of-town speakers. Locals were lucky to be paid $100. The importance of generating income beyond expense was so palpable, we had to budget each prospective course to the dollar. After a while, these calculations became a reflex action and it was natural to think of dollars and cents as a necessary precondition to our scheduling.

It has been my experience that all continuing education programs offering noncredit programs operate in basically the same way, being for the most part, businesses lodged within larger not-for-profit entities. The one major exception is continuing education within a proprietary, for-profit environment. In those cases, adult education is a business with neither apologies nor camouflage. The lion's share of the Smithsonian's revenue comes from federal appropria-

Cash Bug
City Tech

Cash Cow
Smithsonian

Edelson '04

GENUS   CASHUS   CONTINUOUS
         EDUCATION   MAXIMUS

tions. Admission to the museums is free, and it is through fund-raising auxiliary enterprises such as food service, parking, gift shops, and continuing education that additional revenue is generated. The Resident Associate Program was a very visible component of the Smithsonian's business side, paying for itself and then some. We did very well in the 10 years I headed the adult course division (1976-1986) and presented a full range of programs in the arts, sciences, and humanities. Hundreds of thousands of dollars flowed into the Smithsonian coffers, maybe even millions since I was always too busy developing programs to calculate the total take.

With four semesters a year, one term was always ending, about to start, being planned, or being advertised. Thankfully I was young and could maintain this very hectic pace without faltering, even with regular staff turnover. It was a joke among us that people would always be coming and going. The "official" reason was that Washington offered many attractive job opportunities. While true, another big reason was that RAP was an incredibly demanding place to work. Now looking back, from the vantage point of a university perspective, and also after many years, I am in a better position to more accurately assess the workload. The truth is that what we did at RAP was not all that different from what took place at City Tech and in the larger world of noncredit continuing higher education where staff are always measuring their success against the bottom line. This part of our profession has always been revenue-driven, self-supporting, and expected to be profit-generating. And for that reason continuing educators working in noncredit divisions have the most difficult jobs in our profession.

The standards for success and failure are clearly defined. You either made your revenue target or you didn't. Explanations for falling short are viewed as excuses. You've got to do better next time out. It's like being a major sport college coach where the battle for a winning season must be resumed again next year. And as colleges become more and more self-supporting, as a consequence of diminished state allocations and federal grants, the pressure for all forms of revenue generation grows. It is easy to fall into the trap of seeing noncredit as primarily a way to make money, even if I know that this shouldn't be so. Is it wrong to conflate the ideals of continuing education to simply a turnstile philosophy? I used to argue strongly against this; now perhaps I have become more cynical, or just too old to fight?

RAP was clearly the adult education leader in D.C. and we all prided ourselves on the ability to offer the most illustrious speakers on the most riveting topics. Music, art, literature, foreign cultures, science, cinema, current events—we covered the waterfront. If you combined *Smithsonian* magazine with the *New Yorker* and *Time* you would get an idea of our aspirations to be timely, tasteful, and tantalizing. My almost two-hour commute from my home in Laurel, Maryland, gave me the opportunity to regularly comb newspapers and magazines for course ideas. Scribbling notes, underlining passages, ripping out articles, such was my quest for the elusive blockbuster that would pack the house. This challenge of producing an ongoing stream of successful courses frequently stretched my imagination to the breaking point. I had a relentless obsession for success and somehow found the energy needed to keep coming up with good, saleable concepts. In some respects my job combined aspects of Madison Avenue with Wall Street as I tried to consistently conjure up interesting, attractively presented, lucrative subjects.

Bear in mind that these courses were all within the larger category of the liberal arts; that is, nonvocational. Unlike City Tech's career-based continuing education, RAP courses were for intellectual recreation, only remotely concerned, if at all, with what people did at work. We gave adults an opportunity to learn those things that excited their curiosity, or filled a void in their educations. Although non-credit, the courses were taught by well-qualified experts: curators, professors, artists, architects, scholars, and diplomats. The Smithsonian Mall was our campus, and we drew on the abundant talent Washington was known for. At that time, the Woodrow Wilson International Center for Scholars was located in the Castle, giving us access to what in effect was our own think-tank on international and domestic policy. This broadened our curriculum to include world events, diplomacy, and current affairs. Imagine a former astronaut lecturing on the exploration of space, National Gallery curators speaking on their current exhibitions, ambassadors addressing a thorny political issue, visits to the National Symphony as part of a music appreciation course that included a behind-the-scenes tour with Maestro Rostropovich, and you will get an idea of the range and quality of experiences we offered.

It was hard work, always trying to do better than the year before, trying to stay fresh and creative day in and day out. Although about 75% of our offerings were fairly consistent (music, art, archeology, travel, science, the decorative and design arts) we had to always tap new themes and find additional scintillating speakers. I had one program assistant for courses and we tried to split the workload right down the middle. Our routine was to come up with preliminary course lists for the next term and then meet with the

RAP associate director and talk through each course, one by one. The list also included enrollment projections, a budget, special equipment and/or facilities, and, most important, the expected revenue. The refined list would then be reviewed with the director who would also provide suggestions. Sometimes a new course idea would emerge at these meetings. Just as frequently a course would be axed.

This was a spirited give-and-take and I had to be able to defend my ideas and to occasionally reject the ones proposed by my superiors. Sometimes, I went over the line and became more argumentative than necessary. I must confess to several sleepless nights when I thought I had gone too far and feared that I would have to leave. Working at the Smithsonian was a very intense experience, more difficult than anything I have done since. The combination of extremely high standards in a fast-paced, gold-plated work environment, prepared me for anything I would encounter in the future, at least thus far. Looking back I am amazed at my decade-long tenure. That's a lot of courses!

In order to keep churning out desirable programs and survive, I learned to think of myself as the prototypical student: well-educated, middle income, curious about life, with time on my hands, and a desire to socialize with like-minded peers at the Smithsonian. Yes, I tried with all my might to imagine what it would be like to have time, money, and the energy to socialize in the evening after work. Nonetheless, my strategy proved highly successful. And when I recalled my time at City Tech I realized that in order to succeed there I had essentially made the same kind of identification with the intended audience. Although the target groups varied, it was necessary to think about workplace skills, employment opportunities, and necessary retraining from the perspective of the unemployed and underemployed, the bypassed, and the poor.

At the Smithsonian I developed an acronym to help assess the potential success of a program. This was the short and easily remembered word SAM. The letter "S" stood for Status in the sense that we aimed to have high-status speakers or, if not, a high-status topic, for example "The

Country Houses of Great Britain." "A" denoted Achievement since we intended our courses to be serious treatments of an important subject, taught at the university level by superior instructors, ensuring that our students would have a quality learning experience. "M" meant Mystery. This term applied to a range of courses that had a certain drama such as "Mysteries of the Maya" or "Lost Cities of the Middle East." If a potential idea scored high on all three letters, we thought we had come up with a hit, or at least a viable course.

The flip side of success was the dreaded curse of "12": too few students to make a profit and too many to warrant canceling (unless the program had a huge budget; then you had no choice). Of course, if you cancelled a big, elaborate program with celebrity speakers, you could *never* go back to them a second time for another course. So it was important to take calculated risks with the understanding that overall you had to generate each term approximately six high-income courses. We called these "blockbusters." While the typical course enrolled about 25 students, the blockbusters had 200 and up.

I had my share of these huge courses. One was the "Amazing Women of Fashion" organized by Nina Hyde, fashion editor for *The Washington Post*. The course included Sonia Rykiel, Bonnie Cashin, Zandra Rhodes, Elizabeth Taylor, Norma Kamali—high intensity names, to say the least. I think over 500 people attended, packing the Natural History Museum's Baird Auditorium. An analogous program coordinated by Charles Michael Helmken, Chief Graphic Designer at the National Geographic, was "The Creative Genius." This had several iterations, the first featuring top people from the worlds of art and advertising that we brought in from all over the country. I also remember a course on film organized by Richard Brown that had world famous directors and actors. Another course on "The History of Tibet" included a talk by His Holiness, the Dalai Lama. These programs still stand out as stellar examples of what adult education in the liberal arts can be. By the way, we charged approximately $100 to $150 dollars for these eight-week courses. Those with lower expenses had fees of about $65.

In Washington so much revolved around status, real or imagined. This made us vulnerable to those with apparent power or influence, especially in areas we knew little about, or which we had not tried before. It seemed that every other person was an important elected official, a president of a trade association, an influential lobbyist, a famous scientist or academician, or someone closely related to one of the above. Washington, being the center of our national political life, was also home to every nation's embassy. Each country had an interest in shaping the media battle for influence and public opinion. Because our courses were so high profile and attracted an unusual cross section of Washingtonians including politicians, government officials, and military personnel, it became an excellent venue for those who wanted to advocate and "spin" for their special interests. Believe it or not, at the height of the Iraq/Iran war in the 1980s when our government was tilting towards the Iraqis, we featured a course that incorporated an Iraqi fashion show! A comparable program, this time with lectures and a study tour abroad, was organized in cooperation with the Embassy of Sri Lanka. Unfortunately, it coincided with their civil war and had to be cancelled. Another course, developed with the Israeli Embassy, entailed elaborate security arrangements, including the submission of the class roster well in advance. This was all exciting stuff for a Brooklyn boy, with limited prior exposure to the larger world beyond New York.

Janet Solinger, my boss, was in the social whirl of D.C. and often we were asked to follow up on leads with people whom she met at parties, at lunch, or at a diplomatic reception. Sometimes the person we contacted couldn't recall what they had spoken about or more often what they "promised" to do for her. So, one day I found myself speaking to someone Janet had met at a party the previous night. He headed a foundation that promoted the use of solar energy for homes. This was several years after the first oil embargo and there was quite a bit of interest in alternative energy sources during the Carter administration. Perhaps I was jaded about the never-ending queue of people pitching me so-called "blockbuster" course ideas, or maybe it was the lingering memory of my stockbroker course debacle at City Tech, but I had learned to cultivate a perpetual mien of skepticism whenever on the receiving end of someone's brilliant idea. Since my chief had signed on, I had little choice but to go along, trying to make the best of what I had perceived as a bad situation.

In my first year in the job I came to realize that there was such a thing as being too avant-garde for the public who was not yet adequately sensitized to the importance of the subject. No matter how hard we tried, how many pounds of enticing adjectives we used in course blurbs, no matter how "copiously" or "sumptuously" illustrated, no matter how "distinguished," "outstanding," or under the "auspices" of "His Excellency, the Ambassador of —" we sometimes couldn't attract an audience and had to cancel a high-profile program that failed to click. An ongoing dilemma of continuing education is *never* being certain if you are dealing with gold of the highest purity or just another lump of lead.

The title of the course was "The Solar House." Even though it featured a son of Frank Lloyd Wright, it still looked like a big turkey to me. I didn't recognize any of the other names and I was sure that solar energy was just another "within-the-beltway" fad that would be gone tomorrow, like the use of the metric system on Washington area highways and at gas stations. Remember trying to figure out the dollar cost of fuel based upon a per-liter pricing scheme? Bottom line, the course packed our largest auditorium with over 500 seats. A year later, following the practice of Hollywood hits, we did a "Solar House, Part II," also a resounding success. Needless to say I remained mystified by the turn of events. In this case (and also others) I was glad that I had wisely yielded to the enthusiasm of my boss and her friend. In all honesty, left to myself I'm not sure that I would have gone ahead with the proposal. I guess this is what is called following a good leader.

The Price of Success
Another Lesson Learned

It was 1986 and we had just relocated from Brooklyn where we lived in a flat. We were now renting a townhouse in suburban Maryland midway between Baltimore, where my wife Leta worked, and the Smithsonian Mall where I was comfortably ensconced. We were splitting the commuting distance like thousands of other two-income families, each equally inconvenienced! Still it beat the subways and buses of New York and furnishing our little nest was a delightful prospect. Along the way we decided that we couldn't live another day without having an oriental carpet in our new home. But after a few weeks of shopping around, I realized that we both lacked the expertise to make an informed selection from among the hundreds of expensive rugs that were constantly being rolled out before us.

I reasoned that others were certainly in the same straits, so I began thinking about a short course on "The Art of the Oriental Rug." Trouble was that coming up with a great idea is one thing, finding someone to teach it another. In the case of "Oriental Rug" this entailed dozens of cold calls to D.C. area art departments and antique stores until the right person—academic in orientation, but attuned to the needs of rug shoppers and would-be connoisseurs—could be located. I finally discovered a retired professor of art history from a nearby university who was also an avid collector of oriental carpets. Perfect, I thought. In short order the two of us developed a "profusely slide-illustrated" course and an enticing write-up for the newsletter. Continuing educators learn to think in terms of 100-word, adjective-laden blurbs extolling the virtues of a particular course or seminar.

Within days of publication of our newsletter we knew we had a hit. We filled two sections, day and evening, with over 400 enrollees in each. My excitement crested as the registrations mounted higher and high. The instructor was pleased too, not even chagrined (which was unusual) that he had agreed to teach for a pittance. I forget the honorarium; it might have been $60 to $75 dollars for each one and a half-hour session. Finally the date of the first class approached. As was my custom, I always introduced the speaker at the initial session. This gave me a chance to extol his or her notable achievements and to bask in the glory of my ephemeral success as Smithsonian course impresario. That done, I usually took a seat in the rear of the class, settled back, and prepared to enjoy some brief snippets of the presentation before rushing back home. Another justification for only staying a short while, in addition to the long commute, was my own personal connoisseurship of adult education. Much like my new friend, the oriental carpet maven who could spot a genuine antique at 50 yards, I knew what made a good instructor and could tell within 10 minutes of the presentation. In this case, I wished that I had heard him lecture before!

You would think that expertise in a given subject coupled with enthusiasm would result in a well-delivered, informative, and enjoyable class session. You would be wrong. Within minutes I knew I had a problem. I had neglected to determine if the instructor had previously lectured on this theme. Although well-illustrated with slides and actual rugs, the first session was not properly developed for adults just beginning their study of oriental carpets. I drove home fully aware that the next day I would be dealing with a flash flood of phone calls and within the week, letters. Although I had been there before with student complaints, it was never at this order of magnitude. Almost 1,000 disappointed students—including me! The instructor and I had several extensive meetings to discuss organization and presentation. Together we revised the course outline, added an annotated bibliography, severely pruned the number of slides and the net result was that he became a fine lecturer. The damage control worked. I learned two very important lessons. It is far easier to attract and recruit students than to effectively educate them. And, it is a mistake to assume that faculty have prior experience in teaching adults.

This example highlights a critical difference between

adult education and traditional collegiate instruction. We have always been more attuned to student feedback and don't hesitate to step in when things are going wrong. It is an exceedingly short feedback loop between student complaints and our interventions.

Life at the Smithsonian was one exciting day after another. The evenings too for that matter. Because I had networked with so many people I was on many invitation lists for embassy parties and receptions and other similar gatherings. One night in particular stands out. I met Vice President George Bush at a Wilson Center gathering and then later in the evening attended a reception at the Embassy of Indonesia. These were not at all exclusive events, but for me, it was extraordinary. Over time, the strain of days and evenings at work followed by the very long drives home began to take their toll. So I started to look for another job where I could become more of a parent and spouse. I had also been passed over for a promotion and was irked, adding more fuel to the fire. Finding another job, however, was more difficult than I anticipated.

My Harvard "Consolation Prize"

Being passed over for promotion at the Smithsonian really got my goat. After almost 10 years of outstanding program development I justifiably felt I was ready for the next step up which would have been as RAP Associate Director. Beyond the salary increase, the job would have given me the higher level administrative experience I needed in order to land a university deanship and fulfill my long-term career ambition. But additionally, course programming at the breakneck speed we worked was beginning to wear me down. I needed a change.

Earlier in the 1980s Harvard University's Graduate School of Education had created a two-week, residential, Management of Lifelong Education (MLE), noncredit certificate program. This was a boot camp for new deans of continuing education and for others performing similar

duties within different institutional settings such as the
military or not-for-profit agencies. Although not yet at the
continuing education CEO level for which this institute was
targeted, I felt that this would still be a very good thing for
me to attend. By participating with other deans, I could see
how I actually stacked up. Then there were the new skills I
would learn, especially in budgeting and strategic planning.
And last, but not least, I would have after completion a
Harvard certificate under my belt.

One problem: The MLE tuition was expensive, somewhere around $3,000. And there was the additional require-
ment of two weeks away from work. I felt very unsure about
approaching our director for this package which could be
seen as a two-week, all-inclusive, expenses paid Harvard
vacation. In order to bolster my position (new skills, ergo
higher productivity), I came up with what I now refer to as
the "consolation prize" argument. My reasoning was that
although I was passed over for the position I wanted, I was
still a valued, experienced staff member entitled to some
significant show of appreciation. And if I couldn't become
associate director, I should be entitled to a nice consolation
prize, the Harvard MLE. Otherwise my morale would plum-
met along with my commitment to work. And the conclusion of the story is that I attended the MLE and a year later,
Harvard certificate in hand, successfully interviewed to
become dean at Stony Brook University.

Doesn't this seem to justify the reluctance of some em-
ployers to invest in continuing education for employees who
might then subsequently depart? Not really. If you support
continuing education, then you must make sure to also provide challenging work opportunities. Otherwise you will
have trained people to work elsewhere where their skills
can more properly be put to use.

I advise others who are passed over for promotions to
ask for consolation prizes. This, in my view, is a reasonable
request that affords a supervisor a chance to be generous
and reward a staff member who couldn't quite grab the brass
ring. As I see it, the name of the game is to get ahead
regardless of how that may be defined. And you can't con-

vince me that coming away empty handed is a preferable alternative to snatching a partial victory from the jaws of defeat.

Lessons Learned

Success is measured by how well you achieve the objectives set out for you by your institution. In many cases it amounts to cash in the till. To achieve these goals you must identify with your target audience and understand their continuing education needs. Although I have heard that there are places where fee generated income, or some quantifiable entity such as enrollment, doesn't matter, I have yet to personally discover one. Accept the fact that it is a numbers game and move on. Since excellence is always in short supply you will be pleased to discover that high-quality programming very often results in high revenue. Remember that participation in adult education is voluntary and student consumers want the most for their money.

CHAPTER 4

A Return to the Ivy

How to (Not) Interview

I don't know why, but I've had a tough time getting hired. With the exception of becoming Evening Administrator at New York City Community College, all of my other positions were ultimately found after long, protracted, frustrating, ego-deflating searches. It took me several years before being hired at the Smithsonian and the same was true of Stony Brook University. Interestingly, in both cases, I first learned about these vacancies through advertisements in the Sunday *New York Times*. I'm amazed and envious when I'm told how quickly others find new positions. If they are telling the truth, what don't I know? Although by now, it has begun to dawn on me where I tend to go astray and drop out of contention.

It's at the interview where my utter transparency does me in. I just can't seem to conceal my feelings or control my reactions. In case you are wondering, I am the world's worst poker player. So I am outspoken, prone to disagree, and perhaps even standoffish and skeptical. I remember one job interview for a deanship at a university located in Florida. The continuing education office was situated in a trailer, right off campus. At the precise moment I found this out, within the first hour of the interview process, I took myself out of contention to the annoyance of my hosts who had agreed to fly me in and reimburse my other expenses. You should know that several years later the college unveiled a brand new, state-of-the-art adult education facility. But, I just couldn't see beyond the present situation.

CONTINUING Education was in a
trailer outside the campus gate

How could I work in a trailer, especially after 10 years at
the Smithsonian?

At another interview, this time for a college presidency,
I spoke somewhat disrespectfully about state control of

higher education. Little did I know that a representative of the state's Board of Regents was on the Search Committee. Dumb! Looking back, how did I ever find work, especially at the Smithsonian and then at Stony Brook? The answer is that in each case I was fortunate enough to discover that the person I was to work for was temperamentally similar to me. Aggressive, opinionated, stubborn, and for better or worse, totally convinced that he or she was right. Naturally I have to compliment these people on their excellent judgment.

I was very lucky that they took a chance on my succeeding. This was especially true at the point when I wanted to return to academia. My interviewers often found it hard to grasp that the Smithsonian, beyond its exhibition halls and glossy monthly magazine, was also a top-notch academic enterprise, with research projects all over the world. And my work enabled me to interact in D.C. with a full range of university scholars, researchers, members of the diplomatic community, and government officials. Instead, I frequently fielded question after question about the Air and Space Museum or a recent article in *Smithsonian.* Additionally, people who were enamored with the Smithsonian found it hard to believe that anyone would voluntarily choose to leave. I'm sure they wondered what happened; was I caught in the act of playing with George Washington's sword?

Most university faculty follow a common narrow trajectory of undergraduate college, graduate school with teaching or research assignments, leading to a tenure-track university position. Some in the sciences take short-term postdoctoral positions. Except for those teaching in professional schools, it is rare for a professor to have actual work experience outside the university excluding, except for a part-time job back in high school. This helps explain the cloistered, inward-looking stance which, if not exactly hostile to anything beyond the campus gates, is certainly indifferent.

Continuing education by its very nature is one of those university enterprises that deliberately seek to reach over the town/gown divide, serving as an interface between aca-

demic expertise and the needs of the community. It also is
expected to turn a profit on its dealings. Thus, we are twice
tainted in the eyes of the professoriate who are both aloof
from the career needs of working people and condescend-
ing toward those generating funds—much too blue collar
and nonacademic, even if their own familial roots are in the
working class. Of course the irony of highly paid professors
teaching one or two courses per term, trying to limit access
to higher education by working adults who wish to get
ahead, is all too glaring.

Fortunately there is a critical mass of faculty who also
commit themselves to continuing education and its goals.
Without them we simply could not function. But for too
many, outreach and continuing education are marginal activities that take place under the cover of night, on the weekends, off-campus, and now on the internet. One provost even
referred to me as the Dean of Darkness. We are way down
on the list of campus priorities. And though outreach may
be one of the core missions of the college according to its
charter ("teaching, research, public service") and official mission statement, just about everyone knows that this is a
joke. If you disagree, I challenge you to identify the portion
of the campus budget allocated to part-time students relative to their enrollment. Further support for my position
can be found in mission reviews and self-studies required
every 10 years by the regional accrediting agencies. Yet, in
spite of this, the university environment offers wonderful
opportunities for people in our field, and a just about perfect place for program development.

For my Stony Brook interview I prepared by requesting
all the necessary literature on the continuing education program and the university. This was before collegiate websites,
academic databases, and Google searches became common-
place. So I relied on these printed materials, including the
latest edition of *Who's Who*. Sometimes a college president
might be listed, but not always; and hardly ever a provost
or dean. Now it is so much easier to conduct this preliminary research; there are no excuses for arriving at an interview unprepared.

I didn't know anybody I could call at Stony Brook, even in continuing education, since the university had not been active within the national professional adult education organizations. So I drew a blank going in, except for what I could glean from Stony Brook's own publications. I knew it was a unit of the far-flung, 64-campus State University of New York. Some of these schools had technical programs and some agricultural. Stony Brook was terra incognita, although I was aware that it was on Long Island, somewhere in the boondocks. In one of the school's pamphlets I saw reference to a "campus incubator" and simply assumed this had to do with hatching chickens. Fortunately, I didn't reveal my ignorance at the interview when discussion of the proposed "technology incubator" came up. How was I to know? I had never heard the term before. In this respect my cosmopolitan Smithsonian life had its limits too.

During the interview it also became clear that one of the main reasons I was recruited was my experience with noncredit courses at both City Tech and at the Smithsonian. The provost, the person to whom I would report at Stony Brook, had taught at Johns Hopkins University. He knew about the Smithsonian's continuing education courses and when given the opportunity he was hoping that a program of similar quality, breadth, and magnitude could be developed at the university. Prior to the dean's search the campus had invested in an adult education analysis that was conducted by the College Board. This study identified what it thought was a ready market for continuing education courses, especially in the liberal arts, my forte.

The Smithsonian program was able to attract students from the greater Washington, D.C., area including the nearby affluent suburbs of Maryland and Virginia. In this respect the population was comparable to that of other universities positioned in major urban areas, locales that were rich in well-educated professionals with disposable incomes. Stony Brook, unfortunately, was situated in what I came to characterize as a remote zone. Instead of being surrounded by apartment houses with thousands of residents we had millions of trees and squirrels. Needless to say, there were no subways or any other form of mass transit that frequently came to campus unless one counted limited county bus service and a commuter train, the much vilified Long Island Rail Road.

"The Educated Eye"

Noncredit liberal arts were my immediate mandate and I was prepared to do what I had done best, and that was organizing high-class, Smithsonian-type programs with much glitz and glamour. Calling upon my former D.C. contacts we fashioned a program that was a sure hit, or so we hoped. "The Educated Eye" addressed the would-be connoisseur and collector of fine arts, objects d'art, and antiques. It was an all-day seminar (with "sumptuous" lunch) featuring the Honorable Daniel Terra, United States Ambassador-at-Large for Cultural Affairs and also founder of the Terra Museum of American Art in Chicago. Also on this star-studded roster were John Hays, a vice president at Christies, New York, and the well-known collectors Gloria and Richard Manney who had just had a gallery named for them at the Metropolitan Museum of Art. We also had the presidents of prestigious auction galleries in New York, Washington, and San Francisco and assorted additional experts. The program was typical of those that regularly packed the house in Washington. This one played to a full house too, but only because we gave away scores of free tickets! The $95 price tag was too much for a university community that was accustomed to no or greatly subsidized fees.

Of course, the university did have a strong hand, but one it did know how to play. It virtually had the field to itself when it came to low-cost, high-quality, part-time graduate programs for teachers (and aspiring teachers) on Long Island which has a population of about 3 million. These students were served by the university's Center for Continuing Education (CED), at that time the name of my division. Public school educators lacked the "silk stocking" cachet of those who might (but did not) attend "The Educated Eye." On the other hand, they were low-hanging fruit, very ripe for the picking. In fact demand for these graduate courses well exceeded supply! It was a strange situation that revealed to me for the first time the myopia of higher level administrators, and a long-standing, deep-seated bias against part-time students, especially K-12 teachers.

If you can believe it, just 20 years ago public universities in New York could afford to ignore part-time students since the campuses were comparatively generously funded by the state. In those days the universities in New York (and possibly in other states as well) more properly resembled public utilities that were granted a limited geographic monopoly in order to provide a range of public services for an agreed-upon price. There was no competition, except from the private schools. And their tuitions were so much higher, thus leaving the low-cost market to the publics. I remember once speaking with our then registrar and complaining about how cumbersome it was for part-time students to enroll for the summer session, at the time one of my reporting units. Registration was in person, in the Administration Building. And it was on a weekday, between 9 a.m. and 5 p.m., when people would have to take off from work, as well as having to drive (or be driven) to campus. His response, and I remember it so distinctly, was "If they really want to come here, then they have to put up with it."

This type of thinking permeated the institution when it came to part-time students. At its core, the feeling was that if these students were any good they would be here full-time on scholarship (almost all of Stony Brook's graduate students at that time had their tuition paid and also received stipends). Also teachers, in the eyes of university faculty, were overpaid baby sitters who did not deserve the title "educators." Stony Brook's Education Department had been retrenched as a consequence of the budget crisis of the early 1970s (the same one that provided an additional incentive for me to go south to Washington) and teacher education was now just a remnant of this department (see

Rosenthal, 2004). Being housed in the Center for Continuing Education made it clear to the campus community that
teacher education was no longer an academic unit, but just
a service and scheduling function—something akin to the
Summer Session. The university was seeking to reposition
itself as a high-class research institute, albeit one that had
students. Teacher education was lower down on the totem
pole than basic research in the sciences. This was also true
for programs in business and engineering.

These conditions changed by the late 1990s. By then state
funding had been progressively reduced from 70% to less
than 40% of the campus budget. Tuition and research-gen-
erated revenue had to make up the difference. Moreover,
the state's allocation was influenced by enrollment. So having more students, of whatever stripe, was doubly essential (tuition plus state allocation) for the university's fiscal
well-being. So I went from production line noncredit at the
Smithsonian to mass-produced and expanded graduate programs at Stony Brook. A cash cow by any other name moos
as sweet, to paraphrase Shakespeare's *Romeo and Juliet*.

"A Small, Tasty Carrot"

One of the big problems I faced early on was finding a way
to interest faculty in continuing education teaching. The
situation had deteriorated to the point where the number
of courses offered was insufficient to meet student demand.
Students were unable to graduate because the courses they
needed were often not available. Our university had been
founded on what was euphemistically called the "unitary
faculty" principle which meant that professors could allocate their teaching workload among graduate, undergraduate, and CED teaching. Evidently this was more a statement of good intentions than a serious policy, and was more
likely to be honored "in the breach." Moreover, Stony Brook
University does not have a school-wide defined workload
for faculty, so teaching assignments are determined at the
department level, with considerable variation across cam-

pus. In some disciplines a professor may teach one course a
year; in others, as many as five or six.

The problem of encouraging faculty teaching in CED was
originally addressed by Academic Vice President Bentley
Glass, under whose aegis the unit was established in the
1960s. His concept was to create what were to be referred
to as "CED lines," and then to allocate them out to the departments. The lines were to be filled by newly hired departmental faculty whose teaching responsibilities were to
be principally for CED courses. Glass, understandably,
wanted to see CED as an organic and integral component
of the university and its constituent departments. In his
vision, placing CED lines in departments would encourage
the teaching of courses for part-time students without di-
verting departments from their other responsibilities of
research and the teaching of full-time graduates and undergraduates.

Initially more than 38 teaching lines were made available which theoretically could have yielded as many as 40
to 60 courses per semester, based on a load of two to three
courses per faculty. This never came to pass. For example,
one professor told me that when he was initially hired on a
CED line his chair promised him that he would "never have
to teach a CED course." More typically, a department would
honor the commitment, but on a decremental basis. Over a
15-year period, with turnover in provosts, deans, and department chairs, and also CED leadership, the lines were
gradually absorbed into the departments.

By the time I arrived in 1986, we could identify only one
CED faculty line out of the original 38! This generated a
paltry two courses annually for our students. The balance
of instruction was provided by part-time faculty CED itself
hired, independent of other departments and schools. This
policy led to allegations of inferiority. Clearly the whole
process had to be rethought, especially if the school was to
improve its reputation, grow, and take advantage of the
abundant opportunities that existed. A number of possibilities presented themselves. One, advocated by several people
on the provost's staff, was for him to coerce departments to

support CED in return for some favor that they wanted in return. I did not think this approach was workable for several reasons. Once a department found a way to circumvent the arrangement, this would become common knowledge via the campus grapevine and the policy would collapse. Moreover, what was to ensure that competent faculty would be appointed? And finally, perhaps most important from my perspective, if the provost was going to negotiate on behalf of CED, why did he need a dean?

A second strategy, this one proposed by the provost himself, was to hire an independent faculty for CED. I rejected this outright since I was seeking my school's integration with the campus academic mainstream. Also I was afraid that I would never have enough faculty for my needs, especially if the policy of relatively low university teaching loads would apply to this new group as well. Instead, I opted for a third approach. This was a special allocation which came to be called the CED Incentive Plan. The plan, adopted in fall 1987, was simple in concept and easily explained, two essential criteria for success in academic policy making. All faculty appointments in CED, whether full-time or part-time, were to emanate from the academic departments who would take responsibility for the hiring decisions. A $2,400 allocation for each graduate continuing education course offered was made available to the department, regardless of whether the course was taught by a full-time faculty member as part of the teaching load, or by adjuncts that the department hired and supervised. In the case of adjunct hires, departments set the amount to be paid which was charged against their $2,400 allocation.

The most important twist to this new approach, and the feature that made the modest incentive attractive, was that all funds generated by the departments through this arrangement were retained in special accounts managed solely by CED and were segregated from all other department allocations. Department chairs would receive confidential reports on the accounts. Only they could authorize purchases for equipment, travel, honoraria for guest speakers, and other special needs.

By a number of measures the plan proved an immediate success. The quantity and variety of courses quickly increased. Student evaluations of CED teaching quality improved. And significantly, campus perceptions of the school after several terms of implementation were more positive and favorable. I documented these improvements in an article, "Assessing Improvements in University Adult Education Instruction" (Edelson, 1992a). In trying to account for the rapid turnaround, a colleague, observed that the Incentive Plan was a "small tasty carrot" that could be enjoyed by chairs right away. The CED allocations could be tapped day one of each new semester. In the resource-poor environment of Stony Brook University, these discretionary monies effectively augmented departmental budgets. The plan also enhanced the chair's power, another incentive, but of an entirely different kind.

Incidentally, the $2,400 allocation evolved through a series of lunches with many deans and chairs conducted over several months in the University Club. As a consequence of these deliberations, when we went public with the plan we were confident that it would be accepted. Over the years we were able to harness the academic energy and entrepreneurial activity unleashed by this mechanism to launch new advanced graduate certificates and masters degrees. Although subsequent provosts sought to eliminate the incentive with arguments that coercion and appeals to community service would be sufficient, I never considered this a serious position and stuck to my guns. Scrupulous accounting and administration keep the departments happy and we can count on continuity of commitment. In the rare situations when a faculty member teaching a School of Professional Development (SPD) course (we changed our name in the 1990s to more accurately reflect the aspirations of students in degree programs) did not prove up to the task and was poorly evaluated by students, chairs have acted quickly and decisively to find quality replacements. In summary, the use of real-time financial incentives enabled us to exercise much greater managerial and quality control over our programs. I learned that tangible rewards in the here-and-

A small tasty
carrot

Eddis - 04

now were much more effective motivators than promises to
be realized in the hazy academic hereafter.

Looking back to 1987, it is evident to me that the critical elements in developing the Incentive Plan were the nu-

merous meetings and lunches with department chairs. Beyond finding a way of stimulating courses for part-time students, the meetings also identified other topics for joint problem solving. Coming early as they did in my tenure at Stony Brook I was able to forge close relationships with the chairs. This has served me well in subsequent years. I realized that it made sense to get to know people *before* problems develop, rather than only reaching out when in the throes of a predicament. Department chairs are the fulcrum on which the SPD curriculum pivots. Without their interest and support, our gains would not have been possible.

Critics of the Incentive Plan have accused me of bribing departments to support my school (as if that were a bad thing). My rejoinder has been that the financial incentives are too meager to ever be construed as bribes; they simply help chairs and faculty do the right thing. Proof of the Incentive Plan's success has been the adoption of this strategy by others deans seeking departmental support. When questioned for advice, I point out how essential it is to honor commitments. Unless department chairs and faculty believe that there is a 100% commitment to the plan, no incentives will ever be adequate to stimulate change. I am deservedly proud of my reputation of keeping my word and honoring my commitments.

The Incentive Plan's initial attraction was to the most entrepreneurial of Stony Brook's chairs and deans. This group quickly grasped the Incentive Plan's value. It offered a strategy to generate additional resources through graduate programs that heretofore had not been considered central to that unit's operation. For example, Political Science was interested in a part-time master's program directed toward state and county employees. Until now, funds had never been available to address this need. Marine Sciences used the Incentive Plan to generate momentum for an Advanced Graduate Certificate in Waste Management and subsequently a Waste Management Institute. The entire area of teacher education was given a tremendous boost including impetus toward the creation of a full range of Master of Arts in Teaching (MAT) degrees. Once other university departments understood how the plan operated, and what it could make possible, participation across the campus swelled. In the first two years of implementation, the number of CED courses increased from 45 to 89. In recent years the number of scheduled courses has risen to approximately 200, exclusive of contract degree programs which are financed through an entirely different mechanism.

Continuing Education and the Zone of Indifference

Higher education operates on the time-honored faculty principle of the Zone of Indifference. According to this natural law of higher education, the only important thing that matters to faculty is what they do. This means that what you do has no interest for them and is irrelevant unless it either helps or hurts them in pursuit of their private goals. These are usually in the areas of scholarly research and publication and, sometimes, also in teaching. There are a small number of people who become involved with university governance, departmental service, and outreach. They also are the ones the administration regularly taps for committees and task forces. It is a very small percentage of the faculty, thus confirming the Law.

This is not very surprising since the reason most people seek faculty jobs is to be left alone to follow their research interests, to transmit this knowledge to others, and for sabbaticals. To them, time spent in this manner is more important than money, especially if they are at the top of their game as scholars. That is why you will find an infinitesimally small number of these stars engaged in what they view as peripheral activities that will drain away their time and energy. On the other hand, I have found that those stars who teach do it exceedingly well.

The flip side of the Zone for you and me is that we are free to do what we want as long as it stays within the Zone. Since few people care about outreach and continuing education, with the one important caveat of money— which I

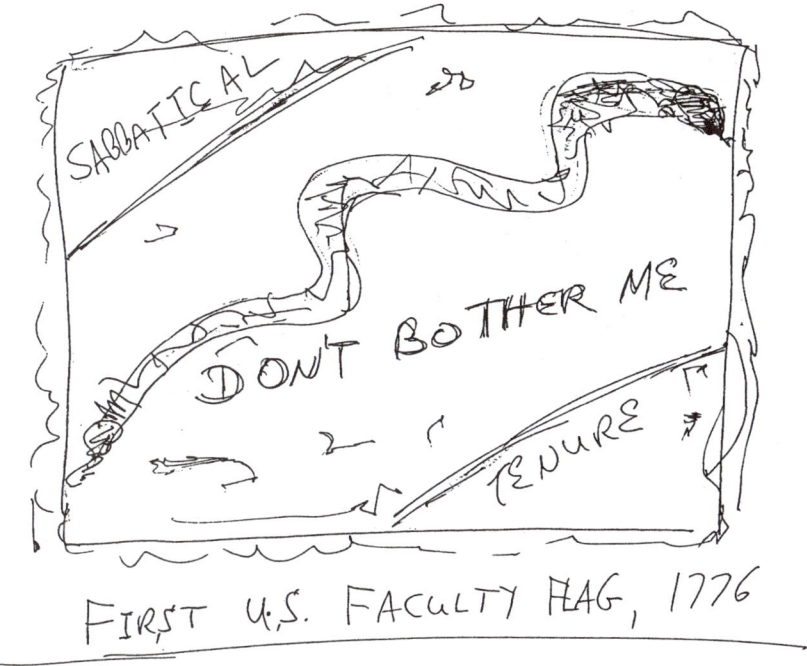

FIRST U.S. FACULTY FLAG, 1776

Edels-'04

will turn to later—it is a place where you can hone your continuing education virtuosity.

Let's assume, for example, out of a list of new potential activities you discover that three of the items are likely to rile a particular faculty member, chair, or dean and would be particularly hard to implement. So you simply move on to other items on your roster, adding new ones as appropriate. You never go back to items 1-3 until they enter the Zone. I have found that recalcitrant chairs and deans eventually cycle out of the rotation and troublesome faculty retire or move on to other schools. They are often replaced by more congenial and/or less experienced folks, and it is then safe to go back to the issues when they are less likely to generate opposition. This approach is also valuable when attempting to acquire more space for your unit, the quest for which, next to parking, is a perennial campus hot button.

But some things may always be too volatile, as I learned the hard way. Because of SPD's success through the Incentive Plan in creating new part-time master's degrees, advanced graduate certificates, and online programs, I felt emboldened to develop a part-time undergraduate degree, the Bachelor of Liberal Studies (BLS). This was a subject that had been floating around the campus for many years without any success. At one time there was also an Undergraduate Evening Program which theoretically made it possible for part-time evening students to earn a degree. It was unsuccessful. The program eventually withered away, creating a window of opportunity for a different strategy addressing the needs of these students.

Through my school's growing interest in online learning I developed a network of relationships with other Long Island deans who were leading their own schools in the same direction. I began to think that online courses could be the necessary dimension that would promote the jelling of Stony Brook's part-time undergraduate degree. I envisioned a collaborative, articulated program with the nearby community college whose dean I had come to know, respect, and like. We thought that both institutions could share half of the necessary degree credits, each relying heavily on e-courses. Online courses would also eliminate the distinction between day and evening part-time students, and allow us to address the full range of this population with greater efficiency.

When I brought this issue to the SPD Council, a Standing Committee of the University Senate that advises me on all aspects of my school, there was strenuous opposition. In a nutshell the consensus was that what individual schools of the university do on the graduate level is one thing, but it was entirely different at the undergraduate. I was warned that SPD would be straying into an arena where many more people had vested interests since the bachelor's degree is emblematic of the entire institution. They would not take kindly to an undergraduate degree that was directed towards what they perceived as weaker students, who would be offered an inferior degree that could conceivably tarnish the Stony Brook brand.

The fears of the Council proved accurate. Although I put together a blue ribbon task force composed of the most respected faculty and administrators on campus, the Bachelor of Liberal Studies project was doomed by a hailstorm of opposition and was heartily attacked in the University Senate. The provost buried the proposal and I can't say I blame him. What I regretted most was not losing, but wasting the efforts of others on this apparently ill-conceived endeavor. I learned a valuable lesson the hard way. I should have realized that I was heading into a very sensitive area (the Zone of Importance) but I mistakenly believed I had the magic touch and would always prevail. The defeat was not incapacitating, and the cause was a good one. Still, I am unlikely to repeat an experiment of this type soon.

Lessons Learned

By choosing to work in one institution, over another, you've made a decision transcending salary, title, perks, benefits, staff size, and so forth. You've selected a set of institutional values that will circumscribe your professional behavior and shape—often without your conscious knowledge—your decision making, how you establish priorities, and how you allocate your time. When you are interviewing, this fine-grained analysis of institutional climate and values is impossible. The evidence is all circumstantial, something that you subtly pick up as you are shuttled from one interview to another. Malcolm Gladwell writes about this phenomenon of thinking without thinking in *Blink* (2005). Using the phraseology of the 1960s what kind of "vibes" do you detect?

At one interview I had at Stony Brook, several of the faculty were wearing shorts. Throughout the entire search process there was very little discussion of enrollment or revenue targets. The emphasis seemed to be on new leadership that would galvanize the university's outreach programs. My instincts told me that Stony Brook would be an exciting place for me to work, with very few shibboleths or sacred cows. It was decidedly not a well-oiled corporate machine like some other continuing education units. Although I was soon to discover that this rose garden had its share of thorns, I knew instantaneously that I'd make the right choice and have never looked back. The moral: when the chips are down, go with your gut, not your brain. Trust me on this. You'll be glad you did.

CHAPTER 5

An Approach to Staffing: Everybody is Special

I still had the issue of redirecting and strengthening the Center for Continuing Education if I was to achieve my goals. All the previous deans in continuing education at Stony Brook had been homegrown from among the faculty. Thus the operation was very inward looking with little reference to the larger professional world of adult education and what was happening in the field. As a consequence, I began a speaker series, bringing in deans and directors from other universities who spoke about continuing education at their own schools. I hoped this would get people thinking about what might be possible at Stony Brook.

I also started reading about the phenomenon of business turnaround. Articles on this topic, and also on leadership, appear regularly in the *Harvard Business Review* and I became an avid reader of that journal. I consider it as essential as anything in the more specialized continuing and adult education journals. The articles are research-based and focused on the real problems of administration and management, and it is a source of information on new books, especially those on leadership and innovation.

How I Hire

One thing I've done in my career is hire a bushel of faculty, administrative, professional, and clerical staff. At New York City Community College I regularly engaged the services of scores of part-time faculty. The same was true at the Smithsonian, with the added dimension of hiring professional and support staff. My unit in the Smithsonian Resident Associate Program was small, consisting of myself as senior coordinator, two assistant program coordinators (one for adult courses and one for studio art programs), a secretary, and a facilities manager. This staff size I later learned was typical of continuing education offices at many small colleges. In fact, I've met many deans and directors who work only with the help of a single assistant.

At the Smithsonian ours was a very egalitarian operation; we all had to roll up our sleeves and do a bit of everything. Usually one term of approximately 100 noncredit short courses was ending, one was in the registration period and would start in another month, and a third was still being developed. I mentioned earlier that this was a true program shop where we were always generating new courses.

During the 10 years that I headed the course division I hired five adult course assistant directors, a replacement just about every two years. At that time Washington offered so many employment opportunities for bright, energetic young people, that after two years working at the Smithsonian, my assistants could just about pick and choose from among those available, often with more pay. So just at the point when I could relax a little and have my assistants share a larger portion of the workload, they were out the door and I had to start the hiring process all over again. The first time this happened I was devastated. And then I came to accept this phenomenon as an inevitable part of administration and Washington life.

Another interesting phenomenon is what I call "The Law of Upgrades." It seemed that I could just about always find a better replacement for the person who was leaving. Now, I can hear you thinking, "*better*, what does he mean?" Each time a vacancy occurred, I had developed a more accurate notion of what that job entailed based upon experience and observation. With the caveat being that this insight was seriously incomplete in that I could never *really* know the entirety of what another person did, even an assistant whose office was literally right next to mine. This is referred to in the sociology of complex organizations as *role ambiguity*. So in filling a vacancy I pared away all of what I regarded as the nonessentials and looked for a very *limited* number of traits.

I looked for people who were enthusiastic, well organized, had a broad-ranging intellect and an appreciation of quality, and were able to act quickly without supervision. If I could be sure of this set of attributes, everything else eventually fell into place. Moreover, I could expect that the unique aspects of the person as an individual would contribute something unforeseen, and often pleasantly surprising to our work. Consequently I approached each new vacancy with scrutiny, guesswork, and in anticipation of how it would eventually be resolved.

With such a strong emphasis on productivity, I realized that liking an assistant was a luxury, and purely secondary to getting the work done. If she or he was effective and we got along, and perhaps even became friends, this was a nice but unnecessary bonus. In fact, it could readily become a deficit if the person's performance deteriorated. As in most, if not all, continuing education bureaus, there was no formal training; it was essentially learning by doing. This was more of a challenge for first-time program assistants with no prior exposure to continuing education administration. These staff members had to find their own way and develop their own convictions as to how the work should be performed. And each person had to achieve a personal sense of artistry, instead of just painting according to someone else's numbers.

A major irony for a soon-to-be dean of adult learning was accepting the limitations of formal continuing education designed to assist low performing and/or poorly motivated staff. I discovered that they either have it or they don't. No amount of remedial workshops could help when issues of personality or character were involved. Improvement is self-improvement and self-directed. It simply cannot be coerced or, worse yet, mandated as a form of punishment.

I always ask at the interview stage if the candidates have read our school's catalogue, when we still published one and, more recently, if they studied the information on our website. You'd be surprised how many people inadequately prepare for their job interviews, even one with the dean. Personally, I can't imagine myself showing up without having learned *everything* I possibly could about the job, the department, and the institution. So when someone doesn't make an effort, I am truly surprised and disappointed. Most distressing, this has happened for senior level candidates. I'm baffled by this lack of initiative and curiosity. On at least three occasions I've stopped the interviews and asked the applicants to go home and study the materials and schedule another time to meet. In two cases the lesson was effective. Both became exemplary staff members.

I won't hire a person, especially a professional, who hasn't prepared by doing the right homework. It doesn't say much for the level of effort they will put into their job. I also take it as a lack of courtesy toward me.

Diversity

Hiring for diversity today evokes broadening the ethnic, racial, and gender composition of staff. Beyond this apt and appropriate meaning, I would like to enlarge the concept to embrace a related usage...deepening and varying the intellectual and talent quotient of an office. It's no secret that we tend to favor and esteem people just like us. The benefit of this approach can be unusual staff cohesion and the ability to quickly achieve consensus on a given subject. The downside of this phenomenon is all too apparent and variously criticized as group think, promoting tunnel vision. But hiring staff that are very much alike in terms of values and traits is understandable. Just think about the counterintuitive behavior of deliberately hiring someone who will always oppose and differ with you and see how appealing that is.

Yet, the rapid rate of change, unforeseen developments in technology, and the importance of quickly identifying new opportunities and capitalizing on them suggest that this responsibility must be widespread within any administrative unit, especially ones like ours where successful adaptation is an organizational imperative. On more than one occasion I've hired someone who was uniquely adept in one sector of responsibility only to later find when the nature of the job changed, say from contract training with business and industry to working with school districts, the person could not or was unwilling to adjust. Of course we all have our limitations and show me anyone who has a crystal ball and can see years into the future. At times, also in fairness to these staff members, I have been unwilling for my own supervisor to alter or add to my own sphere of responsibility.

Understanding that this downside to expertise is possible (if you are an expert in A, you may not be equally talented with B), what does one do? This is a question I have not been able to successfully answer in my decades of experience. I try to look for people with versatility, whose backgrounds show a pattern of success in disparate environments, and who have personally made continuing education an important part of their lives. I tend to favor the hardworking eccentric, who can use the tools of administration in novel but effective ways. Sometimes this backfires, reminding me that predicting a person's success is far from a science.

Another thing, I wish it to be understood that everyone on the staff is an assistant to the dean. I want the novice staff member to know that beyond work-related dedication to a particular unit or bureau, each person holds a separate and special relationship to me above and beyond the immediate job activities. This could entail my asking them to serve on a school or college-wide committee, taking on a very short-term duty (Blood Captain, United Fund Campaign Chair), attending a conference, or doing something else of a related professional nature. I believe for our school to succeed I need to reserve the right to add complexity to a person's job. Still, hiring is and always will be an iffy business, without guarantees. In the present environment of fiscal scarcity every opportunity to hire must be looked at as a precious opportunity to strengthen and improve. I'm afraid that unless you view each search as an attempt to obtain the absolute best you are potentially mortgaging the future of your area.

The Dean's Award for Lifelong Learning

An Achilles heel of all service transactions, including those in higher education, is the "us-them" dichotomy that can, if unchecked, lead to an acrimonious adversarial relationship in which students and administrators see each other as the enemy. Let's face it; this undercurrent of pronounced tension is just below the surface, in most, if not all, economic transactions in our modern world; whether buying a burger, shopping in a department store, or registering for a university course.

I saw evidence of this at Stony Brook when students contacted us with problems. Like all good Long Islanders they would take the offensive, even if they were at fault. And according to the time-honored rules of collegial, hand-to-hand combat, the School of Professional Development staff would make a spirited defense of thrust and parry. I needed to find a way of redefining the way we interacted with our students and thought that if the staff could only perceive themselves as fellow learners this predicament might be solved.

I initiated the Dean's Award for Lifelong Learning. All members of the SPD staff were eligible. The rules were to document a minimum of 100 hours of deliberate study of any subject within the preceding 12-month period, the only caveat being the individual should be prepared to speak about it at the Awards Luncheon. The award was a framed certificate and surprise gift. I was pleased by the number of participants, eventually reaching more than half of the entire staff. This was at all occupational levels and categories, including secretaries, assistant and associate deans, and program managers. The gamut of educational activities ran from taking graduate or undergraduate courses, to library and community book study groups, and informal self-directed study of many varieties.

Over the four-year period, when the award was presented, I had the pleasure of seeing the framed certificates proliferate on my colleagues' walls. I took a special pride in being able to award certificates to people who had never earned them before. The luncheons were fun too when people described what their continuing education had been. An ironic twist was that I was recognized too...with the President's Award for Internal Training (June 1994) in recognition of my "commitment to the professional development of [the SPD] staff."

Now, did the Dean's Award make a positive impact on the quality of our interaction with students? The truthful answer is, I'm not sure, but I would like to believe so. Without question, the award did improve our view of ourselves as a team with mutual respect and opportunity. And it was a morale boost for those recognized. Problems still occur, but I think with a lower degree of intensity. Good customer/student relations are an ongoing challenge. They have to be addressed every day we come to work, not just on the basis of damage control.

Retention

If I have hired correctly, I want to do all that I can to retain the new staff member. And consider the alternative: it might take a full year to replace someone who has just given you two weeks' notice. Since it is a free and open market for good talent, it pays to look closely at how you address this issue. This past year, three of my senior staff, all assistant deans, retired. The New York State early retirement package was too attractive and in each case there was a spouse who had retired several years earlier. Two of these staff had been with me since 1986; the third was my first hire in 1987! I have many other people, both professional and support, with comparable employment records. Why my good fortune?

First, I believe wherever possible, in promoting from within. I'm sure this has something to do with my experience of being passed over at the Smithsonian. Why should I look outside if there is a hard-working, talented staff member who is able to move up? If I don't provide opportunity in this fashion, how can I expect to keep the person if a better job turns up elsewhere? When there is an opportunity for advancement, I resist the desire to hold back a person who is already excelling, in a different role, out of concern that I might not easily find a quality replacement. Giving people a chance to improve and take career risks is for me a moral issue that supersedes any difficulty I may possibly encounter later.

I am also committed to lateral movement within the school and make it as easy as possible for staff to redefine their jobs. Sometimes this leads to temporary frictions, when an individual leaves one office to work for another within SPD. But I am convinced that in the long run this is the best policy since I can retain people within our larger bureau rather than see them go elsewhere on campus. In one case I had to shift a talented person around several times until he felt comfortable and could be productive. It's worth it to optimalize performance. I have to be consistent with my belief in continuing education as a means of upward mobility. Even if losing a staff member to another office creates a huge temporary hole, we have no other choice than a hearty send-off with best wishes for success. Maybe we will be more inclined to work harder to retain the next person who shows an interest in leaving.

Encouraging Formal Education

To my knowledge, I am one of the few deans at Stony Brook who will hire and promote professional staff lacking a bachelor's degree. In some situations I find that a candidate's prior work experience is more important than holding a degree. But mostly my stance is based upon my own personal experience of having dropped out of graduate school and at a later point resuming my own studies at night. I know that this is true for many others as well. Isn't this the obvious reason for any school of continuing education? Looking back, I can point to at least six examples of this policy within SPD.

When posting a vacancy we make sure that having a degree is a preferred but not a required qualification. Why should our school be prevented from hiring the best candidates, even if they lack the sheepskin? But I am pleased if, after being hired, they resume their education because this will increase their value to SPD. In several cases staff members have earned bachelor's and then master's degrees. Since I believe in continuing education, I am an extremely strong advocate within my own school. And perhaps I am revealing a prejudice here; if someone hired lacks the degree, and then does not resume study toward it, I feel let down. I keep asking "How's the degree coming along?" at least once a year, maybe twice. My reasoning is that if I took a chance in hiring they should continue with their studies. Our policy is to provide released time and employees are entitled to one free course per semester. So why not? There are always many valid reasons, as we are well aware. But when I start thinking like this, I begin to question how liberal my ideology really is. Perhaps expectation of the candidate's commitment to continuing education should become a regular part of our search process to avoid misunderstanding later on?

And a Good Time Was Had by All

Having a long-term, dedicated, high-quality staff is of incalculable value. It doesn't happen by accident, only by dint of focus, mentoring, and rewards. I mentioned at a recent conference of my continuing education colleagues that I buy toys for my staff. There was much laughter. But it's true! These vary by the individual and are work related, for example, some new technology, an extra out-of-state conference to attend, books and subscriptions, or office furniture. We also have an active SPD Community Committee that plans holiday parties and unusual retreats. Once or twice we had traditional retreats wherein we were encouraged to talk about work problems. I always left feeling worse than I did before the retreat. So we changed the format to one much more enjoyable. Now the Committee plans a daylong office trip that usually includes a destination of historical or cultural interest, followed by a nice meal. So far we've had tours of Greenwich Village, Ellis Island, and the Lower East Side Tenement Museum, all led by a member of our faculty who specializes in the history of New York; and on Long Island, visits to a vineyard, the Fire Island National Seashore, and the Riverhead Aquarium. These are a lot of fun and we encourage participation by spouses and partners.

Outside of our building is the SPD Garden which we created several years ago, with flowers, trees, and shrubs, benches, and a birdbath. It is a great place to relax and work on that tan. About three times a year we set aside time for weeding and planting followed by an office lunch. The garden contains a memorial plaque for deceased SPD colleagues. By the way, in honor of the three recently retired assistant deans we dedicated a conference room, advising center, and our school's website. It's important to create meaningful traditions of recognition that celebrate collegiality, achievement, and our common humanity. Staffing is the most important thing I do, even more so than budgeting. I can't stress enough its centrality to achievements past, present, and future.

When Staff Do Not Work Out

I head a school of about 30 staff members, about five times larger than my office at the Smithsonian, not to mention a much larger faculty, and student body. Now I can say that everyone here in the School of Professional Development was hired during my administration and that I met every one as part of the search process. But the opposite was true when I arrived at Stony Brook in 1986. Bear in mind that this was my first deanship, a position I had quested for on and off since 1972. I was determined to succeed.

The unit was underfunded, had been led by three different deans in the prior three years, and nobody really knew what the Center for Continuing Education (CED) should be doing, much less how. The staff was demoralized. Under one of my predecessors noncredit programs were suspended. The following year his successor reinstated them. In the Provost's Office the perception was that CED was a bunch of low-performing slackers and not surprisingly I absorbed that view during the search process. Moreover, I was now the provost's new man and had pledged my fealty to his agenda. So I was greeted with trepidation by my new colleagues who correctly perceived that they were under scrutiny and that things would have to change.

Depending upon perspective, I fulfilled either the staff's best or worst expectations. Within the first six months I had dismissed three people whom I believed were either inept or incorrigible. In retrospect I've been questioning these actions. I've seen so much of university administration, the changing priorities, the pettiness, the elitism, the arrogance of tenure, the complete insensitivity to others. I have to wonder if in the larger scheme of things this type of ruthlessness is ever called for? Remember, I had been fired once too, in 1970 or so. I remember when I lost my own job. It closely followed my divorce. I wondered if I could do anything right. Yet, here I was now coming down hard. It's just business, right? Or wrong? It's good to keep wondering about these things. I must always remember that the loss of a job is a personal catastrophe, even if one eventually recovers and bounces back.

But let's be realistic, not everyone works out the way you would like. Unfortunately this may not be apparent until after a number of years of employment have passed following the probationary period. Well, what do you do? A conventional approach which I don't recommend, but sometimes succumb is to doggedly gather evidence, documenting examples of low-grade performance, in preparation for a disciplinary hearing and ultimate dismissal. You shouldn't do this for a number of reasons. First, other people on the staff may support the underdog even if your assessment of their ability is correct. They fear it could happen to them. Second, you give up any chance of the individual working with you to improve once that person realizes that you are constructing a case against him or her. Third, you earn a deserved reputation for being sneaky, further undermining your influence with other staff members.

One of the reasons we follow this course is that we have delayed and failed to adequately address the problem when it was smaller and more manageable. If you find yourself in this bind, back off and gain some perspective. Understand that you share responsibility and approach the ensuing counseling session from the perspective of mutual problem solving. You may be pleasantly surprised at how effective a nonconfrontational meeting can be. Put yourself in the other person's shoes and think about how you would respond to either confrontation or joint problem solving

Another approach is to be direct and use the annual performance review to convey your perceptions. From my experience, this exchange can serve as a real wake-up call, especially when you carefully point out gaps, deficiencies, and expected improvements. Unfortunately most often the annual review is regarded as a time-consuming formality, but there are ways to enhance the value of this mandated activity for both parties.

Several weeks before we sit down to conduct the review I ask my direct reports to make a list of any problems they've had in the past year, what they look forward to accomplishing in SPD, and how I can help them. This list then serves as the basis for a free-wheeling discussion about our office and how things are going. I regard this conversation as much more important than the formally scripted annual review form. There is no substitute for this kind of talk and I like the reactions I have received. The format puts me on the spot too, as a partner and collaborator.

Now what about situations when nothing seems to work? If the staff member is long-term and tenured, your options are a bit limited. Can you simply turn away, chalk it up as a loss, and hope to hire better in the future? Well, yes, sort of. And I'll tell you why. Partly it's my "bottom of the ninth" philosophy which I attribute to Earl Weaver, a former manager of the Baltimore Orioles baseball team. When the Birds were down late in a game with very slim chances of winning, Earl was famous for saying, "Now we've got them [the opposition] where we want them." And the Orioles, more often than not, as least as I remember, came back to win. In my case I like to think that my problem staff person will ultimately surprise me with a base hit, if not a home run. The other more realistic reason is that you've already used your best judgment in hiring this person. And it didn't quite work out the way you wanted. Learn to live with it. It's impossible to have a team made up entirely of all-stars. This is not an argument to intentionally hire poorly. Rather, it is a lesson in humility, to accept that everything is not subject to our personal wills, that everyone has a role to play, and that perhaps, in someone else's book, you are not quite the hot-shot you think you are. Never make it a grudge match, you against him or her. If you do, you will end up diminishing yourself in your own eyes and certainly in the eyes of your compatriots.

For the nontenured staff person whom you believe is unlikely to be awarded tenure, it is best to face up to this as soon as possible and let the person know at the earliest performance review. University policy for nonteaching professionals is to give a year's notice. The staff member has that period to either improve or find another job. I would never delay speaking with the individual once this course of action has been determined.

Lessons Learned

Staffing is the key to organizational success. Always hire the best person available, and if no candidate comes up to your standards, start over again. You need top notch people who will add to the intellectual capital of your bureau. Pay attention to performance reviews. It's one of the best ways I know of helping staff concentrate on their work and what they should be accomplishing. On the positive side, you can use the review to praise achievement as a prelude to additional forms of recognition such as a promotion or raise. Commit yourself to achieving diversity in all forms. Our belief in furthering access and opportunity must first and foremost apply to our own bureaus.

CHAPTER 6
Fitting into University Life

My first priority at Stony Brook was to rebuild the Center for Continuing Education. The successes and setbacks of this challenge were later incorporated in two Harvard Graduate School of Education Case Studies (1987) where I was transformed into the fictional Dean Helen Perotti of Fairhaven University. The cases analyze how the new dean established her credibility and defined a new mission for continuing education within a Research 1 university anxious about its image. Some of the issues addressed in the cases include improving staff morale, establishing a reliable budget for continuing education, generating more programmatic activity, and elevating the position of adult education within the campus culture so that it compared favorably with traditional graduate and undergraduate education. When I look back from a viewpoint of almost 20 years I am amazed at on how many fronts I was active. I must have worked long hours including weekends. What comes across is my conviction that with disciplined focus anything is possible.

This you will surely recognize as another version of the Horatio Alger myth...that by dint of commitment and a relentless application of energy, success is just a matter of time. Alger, however, did not work at Stony Brook University. I think I can legitimately claim a measure of success but not as much as I expected. While I have raised the position of continuing education, achieving parity with undergraduate and graduate instruction has been an elusive chimera. In hindsight this was a far-fetched and inappropriate aspiration as I will discuss later in Chapter 10. Notwithstanding the additional funds we may contribute, adult education has comparatively little to add to national visibility except within the confines of our own profession. Continuing education's frame is more modest and local, measured in the success of each of our students and not in any of the national rankings that are so important these days to presidents and admissions officers.

As Helen Perotti, and in real life, I quickly reached out, entertaining, meeting and greeting chairs, other deans, and influential faculty. Starting with the members of the Search Committee, I probed deeper, seeking to identify allies who could help resuscitate my Center. In addition to hosting one-on-one campus lunches, I entertained weekly at home. These were usually after dinner sherry, cheese, and cracker affairs where my wife and I could get to know others from the university. It might be a couple or an individual, but it was always someone who I believed could assist CED.

This persistent socializing was a carryover from my Smithsonian days where cocktail receptions were de rigueur. But at Stony Brook University, this was something new and different, even a little exotic. I think it was an especially good strategy for the new leader of a unit that had become severely marginalized over the years. Reciprocally, Leta and I found ourselves being invited to various faculty and departmental gatherings where I met still more and more people; in these instances people whom I could persuade to teach in CED.

Another thing I did at the early stage of my deanship was to commission an analysis of perceptions of continuing education at Stony Brook. For this project we contracted with a campus research bureau, the Institute for Social Analysis, located in the Sociology Department. I recall that the study cost $500 and it would have been a bargain at three times the price. When a follow-up study was conducted study several years later I could see our progress. The first study targeted faculty leaders and was conducted by one of the most respected scholars on campus. Beyond providing me with valuable insight on the weaknesses and strengths of my unit, the research reinforced a commitment to change and made this palpable to others within the larger campus community.

A significant finding was that some of the faculty, but not all, who had been at the university the longest were the most critical of continuing education. Newer staff had either a more positive impression due to the new dean, or had a limited awareness of CED. Strategically I decided to concentrate my efforts on younger faculty, and on the senior ones who were positive. So I reached out to those who were neutral and positive in order to expand CED's base of support, trusting to attrition and retirement to take care of the negatives. This proved to be sound logic, and as the years passed on, so did most of my critics. I find now that those currently having low impressions of continuing education do so because of ideology, not out of experience. And I find this snobbism easier to ignore while I continually work at expanding our base of active support.

The provost provided me with generous funding, although at the time I failed to fully grasp its significance. He bought into the Incentive Plan which succeeded beyond our mutual expectations. He also kept me fully involved with many aspects of the campus academic program including participation in the tenure review of faculty. I did not appreciate how exceptional this was for a university Dean of Continuing Education. I was also involved in high-level search committees and enjoyed full cooperation of his staff in the areas of staffing and budgeting. Little did I realize that this special relationship would not carry over to his successors. Unlike the Smithsonian where senior administrators seemed to stay in their jobs for decades, the life of a university provost is precarious, with an apparent half-life of about three plus years. Each new incumbent developed his own priorities and plans. And the fortunes of the campus deans varied accordingly.

As soon as my first provost stepped down and was replaced, my access and importance waned dramatically. I was now on the outside looking in, while newer deans temporarily occupied positions of privilege. The premises of the

Incentive Plan and its modest allocations were contested as the university entered a period of economic adversity in 1989 from which it has not yet fully recovered. The fighting over resources intensified and we all began to participate within a contentious enviornment where we jockeyed (even more than usual) for influence and opportunity on behalf of our respective schools and colleges. My reading material now included works by Castiglione, *The Book of the Courtier* (1959), Machiavelli, *The Prince,* (1980), Clausewitz, *On War* (1989), and Sun Tzu, *The Fine Art of Making War* (1983) in addition to the conventional literature on leadership and strategic planning. I was determined to fight and resist any possible assaults on my school. Fortunately, I did not stand alone and could count on a growing cadre of supporters.

The SPD Council

The School of Professional Development (SPD) Council is the most useful asset I have in advancing the cause of my school. Technically it is a Standing Committee of the University Senate and is "advisory to the dean" on all aspects of SPD policy. We meet four times a semester, for a little over an hour. The meetings, consisting of a brief update from the Dean and subcommittee reports, are deliberately short and focused to ensure that we address the most important issues. Depending upon need, there may be additional meetings of smaller work groups throughout the term.

The Council's significance derives from the way the School of Professional Development is staffed. Like most university continuing education units we do not have full-time faculty located in our school. We use part-time adjunct instructors or faculty sited in other academic units, departments, and divisions to teach. Our core staff therefore is either professional or support, the distinction usually hinging on level of education, salary, and the demands of the job. The support positions are either secretarial or clerical and tend to be generic to the university environment. Not so with the professional jobs which are usually highly specialized. It would not be uncommon to find in large continuing education units scores of program coordinators, a dozen senior level managers, a clutch of assistant and associate deans, and also strong staffing in marketing, budget, and personnel, but rarely full-time faculty.

This pattern of staffing coupled with the fact that nowadays the dean/director does not ordinarily come out of that university's faculty, as it did in the past, means that there is now very little in common between continuing education, as an administrative unit, and that of academic departments and schools. Continuing education tends to resemble more closely other administrative units that interact with academic subsystems such as enrollment, finance, alumni, and some types of campus auxiliary services. But, with one crucial difference; that being continuing education's role in developing, administering, and evaluating a varied range of academic programs, credit and noncredit.

The absence of full-time faculty in continuing education minimizes our division's influence within the full range of academic decision-making bodies such as committees on curriculum, promotion and tenure, and campus academic policy. The Faculty Senate, on campuses where it exists, is the most august of these committees. And, even in cases where full-time professional staff are also voting members of these groups, my perception is that they are *not* as fully enfranchised as faculty.

If your continuing education unit has responsibility for developing and administering academic programs including granting academic degrees, how can you ensure the appropriate level of faculty involvement comparable to what would obtain within an academic department? To maintain academic integrity in curriculum planning and evaluation, faculty hiring and supervision, adjudication of student petitions, and addressing issues of student academic policy, it is essential that parallel and effective quality control mechanisms exist. One approach is to defer responsibility to the appropriate academic departments that provide the courses, or to preexisting pan-college review bodies for either undergraduate or graduate studies. Yet by following this course of action, the continuing education unit can *never* develop its own academic infrastructure and the deep feelings of ownership for its programs. On the other hand, were the unit to create these internal decision-making bodies and staff them with its own professional, non-faculty staff, they would lack the academic respectability and provenance necessary to legitimize its decisions. The SPD Council offers a strategy for academic accountability within continuing education, and a means for achieving important linkages with the university's academic mainstream.

Members of the SPD Council are elected for overlapping three-year terms by means of a campus ballot administered through the University Senate. This group usually consists of faculty and professional staff supportive of SPD. I augment these elected representatives with my own appointments representing units whose participation I judge important to my school. Typically this includes department chairs whose courses are integral to our degrees, heads of administrative units such as admissions, counseling, institutional research, and often a member of the Provost's Office. The broad composition of the Council, representing a cross section of the campus, both academically and administratively, has made it an extremely efficient venue for discussing problems, brainstorming new ideas, and of course conducting business.

Faculty who participate in the Council can subsequently bring issues which we discuss to the attention of other bodies on campus and act as our advocates with other deans, the provost or president, on behalf of the school. Recently, long-term members of the SPD Council, who have also spent time teaching SPD courses for their departments, became associate deans within other schools of the university (Arts and Sciences, Marine Sciences). A third serves as Associate Provost. Their familiarity with SPD activities and priorities helps with intracampus communication and cooperation. Since the Chair of the Council sits on the Executive Committee of the University Senate, I also have an alternative means of raising issues of importance for consideration by the campus community.

One example of the Council's value occurred when our school was exploring the desirability and feasibility of online graduate courses and ultimately a degree. This subject received a rigorous yet timely review by the Council which enabled us to quickly move forward. Try to imagine how this type of proposal would fair had it gone through traditional academic channels. More than likely we would still be talking about it five years later. In my experience, most academic bodies exist for deliberation and only secondarily for decision making. I make this observation in fairness, not acrimony. If we are to act and implement we require administrative mechanisms compatible with the here-and-now continuing education culture.

I consider the Council exceedingly beneficial to the School of Professional Development and encourage you to explore and develop similar governance structures. An additional personal observation: provosts and presidents cannot so easily avoid addressing the concerns of full-time faculty who make themselves heard in the open forum of university senates. This is another way of amplifying the volume of your messages within a noisy campus environment. Hear, hear!

Stickball and Community at Stony Brook

Joining Stony Brook was something of a homecoming for me. After 10 years in Washington, which John F. Kennedy famously referred to as a "city of southern efficiency and northern charm," I was finally back on native soil. During my interviewing I even came across a number of fellow Brooklyn College graduates. It turned out that the campus was full of them for the simple reason that Long Island was only a short drive east from Brooklyn, and offered all the benefits of the suburbs coupled with convenient access to the New York metropolitan area. Just so that you don't get the idea that our university was parochial, we also had many former residents of Queens, the Bronx, Manhattan, and even Staten Island, New York's smallest and most remote borough.

Most of us who claimed New York as our hometown also shared a range of formative youthful activities such as schoolyard basketball, street roller skating, and stickball. This latter, and to my knowledge, unique New York sport is played with, not surprisingly, a stick (broomstick) and a hollow rubber ball. The end of the stickball bat was usually wrapped in black friction tape in order to avoid splinters. Although specially manufactured so-called "regulation" bats appeared on the market, in my mind there was no substitute for the hand-crafted model.

Stickball has two major variations or genres: distance and pitching. The former is usually played in the street, or gutter; the latter, in a schoolyard having a concrete handball court. The object of distance is to hit the ball as far as possible measured in manhole covers or sewers. A sewer is a homerun. Two sewers is a Herculean blast. In pitching, a strike zone is painted on the handball court. The opposing pitcher tries to strike out the batter as in baseball. Hits are based on distance. In both variations ground balls can be fielded. Do you really need to know these finer points? Probably not. I just want you to be aware that stickball is viewed as serious sport.

I began to ask among my colleagues if any were interested in playing stickball? Within a very brief period of time we identified more than a sufficient number to begin. For about a year we assembled on campus Saturday mornings from 10 a.m. to noon. This was time enough to play several games alternating sides. At one time a dozen faculty and administrators took part. This was a goodly number and made for plenty of team variations. As word of our games spread, more and more people began to show up as both fans and critics. I wrote a humorous article, "Reliving the Simple Joys of Stickball," which appeared in the Sunday *New York Times* (March 26, 1989). And of all my writings this one continues to elicit the most interest especially among former New Yorkers and Brooklynites. Playing stickball helped me become part of the larger Stony Brook team. But first and foremost it was fun and gave us all the opportunity to revisit some of the most pleasant moments of our youth. We had nicknames. I was the "Commish," short for Commissioner.

Looking back to my participation in these games, I see an exuberance that would be hard to duplicate now. Sure, I'm older; but it's more than that. I've become more serious and guarded. And when the weekend comes around, I'm less inclined to return to campus, even for sports. I think a lot of my enthusiasm for stickball had to do with being new, and being able to come up with an exciting idea that could capture others' imaginations. I'm willing to bet that opportunities like this still exist here, waiting for someone to tap into. A few months back I saw some of Stony Brook's international students playing cricket on our stickball court. I walked up and casually asked if I could play. I am guardedly optimistic that my stickball skills will translate into this similar sport.

Stickball has provided a means of displacing some of my competitive energies. My will to win is very strong and at times I have been known to bend the rules in my own favor. This is true for *everybody* on campus, nullifying anyone's individual advantage. You need skill, determination, and a little bit of guile both on and off the court. This is what stickball teaches us.

Provosts and Presidents

Since coming to Stony Brook University I have served five provosts and two presidents. For those unfamiliar with campus terminology, the provost may also be called the academic vice president or AVP. Typically the provost is the senior vice president, the first among equals, in the same way that the dean of arts and sciences is compared with other campus deans.

The provost serves at the behest of the president and holds a subordinated position like that of deans relative to the provost. A significant difference is while deans have line managerial responsibility for their schools, provostial power is exercised over a much larger academic area. For that reason it is both greater in span, but much less in the understanding of specific details. In the best of circumstances, provosts work through the campus deans who are expected to have a fine-grained knowledge of their respective spheres. Even so, a dean of arts and sciences may be responsible for 60 departments, having only a smattering of knowledge in some disciplines. The intellectual pitfall for all administrators with wide-ranging spans of responsibilities is to believe that their extended domains of control confer upon them superior knowledge, even more so than those with direct hands-on responsibility.

Provosts, unlike deans who must account to department chairs, have a direct report to the president and thus have a sharply focused answerability to a single person. They are also viewed by the faculty as their advocate. The potential for significant conflict in these two aspects of the provost's role accounts for why they come and go with such startling frequency, even though the job is reputed to be the second most powerful on campus. By my own observation, it is a popular myth that provosts go on to be presidents. Of the five I have worked for, only one thus far has been able to snatch this elusive prize.

Deans of continuing education have a unique challenge when dealing with their AVPs who traditionally are hardcore academics, most having previously served as chairs or deans. I was fortunate to report to a provost who personally taught and encouraged other senior faculty to teach graduate courses in SPD, but this is rare. Usually provostial incumbents are steeped in their disciplines, with barely an inkling of knowledge about continuing education. If they do think about it, their notions may be fixed by whatever form continuing studies took at their former campuses. Also, the type of relationship they had with the continuing education dean or director at their old place, not always favorable, may be transferred to you. So it is a good idea to call and check with your continuing education counterpart at the other institution whenever a new provost arrives. Even if the news is bad, you at least now know what to expect. If the provost is promoted from within, you have a track record to examine and many people with whom to speak and compare notes. It is one of my personal laws that people behave true to form. Prepare yourself.

I remember a phone call I made about a newly anointed provost. My respondent dolefully reported that he had been a "continuing disappointment from day one" and "always lied." Could this be the same pleasant person I met during the search process? Sad to say, it proved to be true to the letter. Eventually the person left and I had to begin anew with his replacement. A word of advice: if you decide to become a dean or director of continuing education, you must resign yourself to this seemingly endless and frustrating cycle of re-educating the new provost. But at least lifelong learning is our business and we should be better at it than the next person.

So I said to the provost "Take as much $ as you need." And he did!

Edelson 04

One interesting thing I've observed is that for the provosts I've worked with at Stony Brook, the discipline makes the person. One provost's field was marine sciences, a very interdisciplinary area with much interaction with the public. I'm sure this influenced his acceptance of the interdisciplinary Master of Arts in Liberal Studies, SPD's most popular degree. A provost who was an economist saw us strictly in financial terms, valuable at the margins. And a historian had a difficult time with the amorphous nature of continuing education and its unpredictable evolution. A research biologist was troubled by the absence of precise knowledge, especially in continuing education decision making which is often based upon gut instinct in lieu of detailed analysis. Also his strict notions of academic hierarchy placed us at the bottom, way below other departments and divisions. This was a difficult time. Yet, I was able to hunker down, grow my budget, and stay the course. Still, it was a close shave with disaster. When other deans share their tales of woe I've got plenty with which to reciprocate.

Presidents

In my view, campus presidents are like exalted potentates. They live far away in a castle and occasionally make a royal visit to their outlying dominions. If you are doing a good job, they can tap you on shoulder with words of praise. But if you require some cash, they invariably refer you to the local baron or provostial lord. The one exception being your request for a "royal boon" as in: "A boon, sire, if it pleases Your Highness."

A number of years ago we were just starting to investigate online learning. It was a new area and, although a few universities had already developed virtual courses, the know-how was not as widely distributed as it is today. So we had to experiment, and following the advice of Peter Drucker and his advocacy of puny experiments (1993) we diverted small amounts of our budget to this project. I convinced an SPD staff member who struck me as the most comfortable with computers and the internet to spearhead the effort. We began by hiring as an adjunct faculty member a person who was then currently teaching an online course at another New York college. We started with the two courses that she taught, and then moved up to five with additional faculty, and then to ten, and so forth, progressively increasing our internal budget reallocation as the demand for these electronic courses continued.

All along I had been briefing the provost about this project and its exciting expansion, asking for additional resources. Although he appeared to champion innovation, he never to my knowledge backed it with funds. This continued for several years. Finally I couldn't take it any longer. We didn't control sufficient resources to keep growing the program and I was at my breaking point. In one of our meetings I demanded, "Do you support me or not?" He signified in the affirmative. To which I responded, "Well, will you finally give me the money I have been asking for?" His response this time was unambiguously negative. I asked him why. His explanation was that he wasn't 100% confident in me or online education! "Fine," I exclaimed in exasperation, "then I don't want your support" stalking out.

The problem was that I had a tiger by the tail in the form of rapidly expanding online enrollments and refused to discourage growing student demand. I had no choice but to avail myself of the ultimate dean's prerogative which is to see the president. I had done this once before with President John Marburger when I had a problem with an earlier provost. The president convened a meeting and enjoined us to work in harmony. Nothing really changed and eventually the provost was replaced. I am sure this emboldened me to try again several years later with a new provost and president. This time good fortune prevailed. My request for a boon, actually on bended knee, was rewarded with a generous allocation. Shortly thereafter the provost was replaced.

Now before you go charging off to what may be your personal Waterloo, consider all of the consequences, the potential upsides and downsides, and how confident you are in your own judgment. It is not simply a case of having chutzpah, although this helps. More important you have to know your subject, the protagonists, and have an honest appraisal of your own track record. I'd like to believe that the president's support of online education was based, in addition to the merits of the case, on my professional reputation. This is what it usually boils down to in the long haul.

The University Club as a Second Office

At the Smithsonian our campus eatery was in the Castle. This 19th-century national landmark building was designed by James Renwick. It had stained glass windows, Belgian tapestries, even resident barn owls in the castle towers. On one occasion I climbed into the tower to take photos of the little, newly hatched fledglings. The pictures were subsequently published in the Smithsonian newsletter. We had a chef and a bar...what a great and elegant setting! Taking guests out to lunch there was a mutual treat. And having a luncheon charge account in the Castle was a very nice perk.

By way of contrast, Stony Brook's campus restaurant was very run down at the heels. There was one memorable lunch I had there in my first year with President Marburger. Right after we sat down at our table it toppled over with a resounding crash! It had been broken the evening before by students who were no doubt in a very celebratory mood and was precariously balanced with about 20 matchbooks. When we sat down, our vibrations were enough to set off the collapse. Jack didn't bat an eye. We simply moved to another table and resumed our conversation without missing a single beat. This was an amazing demonstration of sang froid that I marvel at even today.

The next year the University Club officially opened. The driving force, not surprisingly, was a new provost who had come from Johns Hopkins where they have an outstanding club. The provost envisioned a comparable establishment, and though it does not rival the Hopkins club in elegance, I can honestly say that it has evolved as an important feature of campus life. In addition to serving lunch, it is a choice venue for departmental parties and receptions.

Following up on my practice developed at the Smithsonian, I arranged for an open account and my personal table by the window. I then began regularly taking to lunch faculty, other campus administrators, students, and guests from off-campus. The Club has helped me solve the thorniest problems, calm the most troubled waters, and win friends for SPD and the university. My reasoning is "I have to eat anyway, why not have a good meal, in a pleasant setting, and get some work done too?" I'm told that the University Club runs at a deficit which doesn't surprise me. Colleges seem to be unable to run things efficiently. Depending upon your values, this is either deplorable or a virtue.

During the summer the Club is closed and I metaphorically move my table to the cafeteria in the Student Activity Center (SAC). This is a wonderful setting too for meeting and greeting, catching up, and initiating. I'm sure every college has some place that can serve the same purpose. I love being able to run into people at the SAC or the Club

Every Campus Has a Place to Meet and Eat

and at the same time move my business along. On a campus these restaurants substitute for the cocktail parties that are ubiquitous in Washington and enable one to share information and shore up relationships that may have become strained in the rough and tumble of doing business.

Lessons Learned

Nothing comes easy, especially in continuing education. Focus and incredibly hard work should see you through most situations. Get to know as many of your university colleagues as you can. This network of contacts will pay big dividends when you need to enlist others in achieving your continuing education goals including routine issues like staffing committees and task forces, and, of course, teaching in your school's programs. Become part of the campus in ways that are natural to you.

Put up with the provost. Somewhere along the line you will find one who is intelligent, friendly, has continuing education as the first university priority, and always agrees with you. Snap out of it. Daydreaming like this will get you nowhere!

Regarding your boss, most provosts will let their new deans get away with murder the first year. By year two you should have figured it out, otherwise start looking through the *Chronicle of Higher Education* for your next job.

CHAPTER 7
Leadership in Continuing Education

Roots of a Preoccupation

My interest in leadership dates back to my grade school years. There was a period when I was obsessed with mailing away for free offers. As a consequence, one day I received at home a large carton containing several file boxes and at least a hundred 6" x 8" index cards on leadership development. It was my first continuing education course! Being 11 or 12 at the time I was definitely nonplussed, especially when the accompanying materials informed me that subsequent lessons, for which I was already preenrolled, would require me to spend what was then a hefty amount. It was greater than what my parents allocated to me for stamp collecting.

Fortunately I got my Dad to intervene and cancel the program without penalty. But not before I was exposed to what I later learned was a variation of simulated "in-basket" exercises, which were then in vogue as a form of leadership development. I was to encounter this training technique again when I was in New York University's Higher Education Doctoral program. By that time, this mode had evolved into a heuristic device for sharing perspectives, rather than being seen as a way of identifying the single "correct" response from among several other choices offered on the card.

As soon as I found myself supervising people, beginning with my job at City Tech, I started reading about and studying leadership. My doctoral dissertation was on the role of the department chair in higher education, so I was already steeped in studies of role analysis and other facets of the sociology of complex organizations.

My strategy in keeping up with the burgeoning leadership literature is to immediately order new books as soon as I see them advertised. Otherwise I forget. By the end of each semester I usually have at least a dozen unread books in the corner of my office. I used the winter intersession and summer vacations to plow through them. I also usually arrange to be giving a workshop, seminar, or conference presentation on leadership at least twice a year. So I have the ongoing challenge of reading and interpreting new material and of sharing these ideas with others. Now, of course, the million dollar question is, Am I a better leader after reading and teaching about leadership? Of course! But kidding aside, I can't think of a better approach than reading, reflection, teaching, and application followed by further reflection and still more reading.

Some of the books I've benefited from include Maccoby's *The Gamesman* (1976), his more recent *The Productive Narcissist* (2003), Wheatley's *Leadership and the New Science* (1994), and *Primal Leadership* (2002) by Goleman, Boyatis and McKee. I explored leadership for our field in *Rethinking Leadership for Adult and Continuing Education* (1992) and with Joe Donaldson contributed a chapter on this subject to the *Handbook of Adult and Continuing Education* (2000).

My personal leadership journey has ranged from left brain to right brain, and everything in between. I've studied the rational and humanistic approaches, theories x, y, z, interactional and incident based approaches, systems theory, chaos, charismatic leadership, and on and on. And on. So let me couch the following observation within this rather complex background of layer upon layer of reading. The single most important issue for leaders today is **innovation.** That is encouraging, recognizing, rewarding, evaluating, rethinking, and responding to the need for change *with* value.

I can't think of anything more important. Once I've hired the right people and they've become competent in fulfilling the core duties of their jobs, I expect them to innovate, to challenge, to reconfigure, to streamline, to push out from where they currently are. A good book addressing these issues is *The Individualized Corporation* by Ghoshal and Bartlett (1999). I see our work in continuing education as no more than a series of experiments, some running longer than others, from which we learn and design new experiments. Easier said than done, especially when someone on the staff challenges what has become your own sacred cow.

For example, prior to publishing a single source catalogue for all of SPD's continuing education programs, each separate unit had its own fliers, pamphlets, and posters. There was no single place to see the entire array of offerings, not to mention the out-of-control mailing and printing costs. The new unified School of Professional Development catalogue was a vast improvement. But my satisfaction with this innovation caused me to become resistant to suggestions of moving to an online publication. I imagined all sorts of dire consequences, especially a decline in enrollment if we were to abandon direct mail. Finally Patricia Baker, a very confident staff member, went ahead and decided the issue herself. The online catalogue has been a great success and I'm glad the decision was made for me. I was unable to see the potential good and instead overly dwelled on what I imagined to be negative outcomes.

In my workshops on innovation I review America's love/hate relationship with innovation and invention, and the considerable barriers innovators face. I'll just mention a few – fear of failure, fear of change, fear of others and what they might think. There is often a preponderance of downside thinking because it is easier to anticipate the problems of implementing something new and untried rather than any possible benefits. This resistance prompted *Enhancing Creativity in Adult and Continuing Education* (Edelson & Malone, 1999).

From Acorns to Oaks

Peter Drucker, as I mentioned earlier, advocates small experiments. He argues that when the stakes are low, success and failure do not loom as large as either incentives or disincentives. A comparable approach is the 3M Corporation's philosophy of "make a little, sell a little" (Ghoshal & Bartlett, 1999). Very few of us have the resources to undertake large-scale innovations in our continuing education bureaus. I tend to follow an incremental strategy or from the "acorn to the oak" as I often refer to this approach. And when successful, this allows me to move winning ideas from the periphery to the core of our school's portfolio. I can give you five good examples of puny experiments that flourished into a mighty grove.

1. **The SPD Incentive Plan**. Chapter 4 describes this innovative way to stimulate faculty to teach in SPD. When first initiated we sponsored approximately 50 courses. This has grown to nearly 200 each term.

2. **The Round Table**. This began in about 1989 as a small informal meeting held in my office with several retired friends of Jo Fusco, who was then our Associate Dean. I explained the concept of Institutes for Learning in Retirement (ILR) programs based upon what I had learned about American University's ILR when I worked at the Smithsonian. Now the Round Table is a robust, peer-directed, learning society with over 600 very active members.

3. **The Electronic Extension Program (EEP)**. Eight years ago we began with 2 graduate courses per term and now offer about 70 serving approximately 1,400 online students each semester including summer. Online courses have become an integral part of our program. We present an entire master's degree online and intend to augment this with additional degrees and certificates in the next few years.

4. **Certificate Programs for School Administrators**. Approximately 700 matriculated students are in these graduate certificate programs which commenced about six years ago. This also began as a small pilot program that subsequently took off.

5. **Contract Courses with School Districts**. SPD delivers off-campus degree programs to local school districts and teacher's centers. They are held all over Long Island in 20 different locations.

Failed experiments abound too, as in the case of small programs that either got smaller or stayed the same size. I can cite graduate certificate programs in Long Island Regional Studies and in Environmental Occupational Health and Safety, and a noncredit, free community outreach program called "Coffee and Conversation" we sponsored on Friday evenings for several years. I was reluctant to cancel this free series, but in this case had help from my provost, who thought the program wasteful of resources. He was right in the sense that the expenses were greater than the revenue....since there was no income. But I argued, apparently unsuccessfully, that there was a place for free programs and not everything we do in continuing education should carry a price tag. We have also miscalculated with two Advanced Graduate Certificate programs in Operations Research and in Industrial Management. These were conceived by academic departments without any sense of potential audiences.

My best advice is not to go along with an ambitious initiative until you are firmly convinced that it is worth allocating the considerable time and effort it takes to bring an idea to fruition. In our case, a full-blown degree proposal is required, in addition to state approval at two layers: the State University of New York and the State Education Department. Why go through all of this without any plausible evidence of demand? I've noticed that faculty are very good at writing proposals stemming from their experience in seeking grants. It is important to remember that no matter how well written or brilliantly conceived an adult education program may be, if it is not designed and targeted for a living, breathing, and willing audience, it is a waste of everyone's time. What's the point of listing degrees and certificates in your brochures and web site if they are not viable? Avoid academic Potemkin Villages which create the illusion of activity and enrollment without the substance to back it up.

Significant improvements have been made in the way we use our school's website for orientation, advisement, registration, and marketing. This is the way students learn about us and hopefully decide to select one of our programs. Very often I log on myself, trying to see how well we are informing the world about SPD.

I'm sure that you can point to comparable improvements in your own programs. Yet if you have ever worked for cautious, fear-of-failure supervisors, who never have enough data to make decisions and are scared stiff of having to advocate on your behalf, the different environment sketched here should be palpable. Sometimes we've implemented decisions that have flowed up through the ranks which didn't work out. So we canceled them once we realized they were not producing the intended results. What is the point of dwelling on failure, other than to depress future initiatives? Since that is not my goal, I favor Drucker's approach of low threshold stabs at making a better future.

Returning to the application of technology to education (radio, television, satellites, fiber optics, video, etc.) there have been so many instances of overselling and over-promising innovation, leading to disappointment and disdain. Yet, without exaggeration, online learning has been a significant success. My strategy was to become an "early adopter" and quickly work through the learning curve so that I could take advantage of new iterations of the technology as they came out. From a budgetary perspective it is important to realize that within colleges and universities there is always fierce competition for additional resources.

Coming forward with a timely proposal undoubtedly aided my advocacy.

Can you be an effective leader without engendering innovation? No. On the other hand, change simply for the sake of change, sometimes referred to as novelty, is not a sensible strategy. Keep trying to increase educational value for students and your institution through deliberate change. Ongoing innovation is also good business, fiscally speaking, in the acquisition of new capital. Our field is one of flux and change. If you are not trying to be in tune with what is going on, you will unfortunately miss many opportunities to drive your unit forward. Above all, seek to release the creative and entrepreneurial energies of your colleagues and free them from the yoke of obsolete traditions.

In this vein, I had a memorable discussion with a Stony Brook professor who was a recipient of the MacArthur Foundation's genius award. I asked him if he thought there was a downside to encouraging everyone's creativity and was taken aback by his response. He maintained that a general policy of promoting creativity would encourage chaos, undermining organizations and society. Although I disagree because he is an officially certified smart person, I can't simply dismiss his position. From my perspective we need more creativity, but rigorously evaluated, in order to sift novelty from change with value. How can encouraging this be a bad thing? And if we were to restrict the ability to innovate, whom would we exclude, and would we not miss out on many great ideas? Then again, he won the "Big Mac" and I haven't.

According to Howard Gardner in his creativity research (1983) it takes about 10 years to master a particular domain or area of interest. So it is important to realize, especially if you are just starting out, that your most noteworthy contributions to the field of continuing education are yet to come. A commitment to innovation entails a willingness to reexamine all aspects of your programs, including the assumptions underlying operations. This should address the reasons why certain programs are offered and also why some are not.

The Innovation Check List is a good way of thinking through possible changes. But don't be limited by it. You might find that talking through rough ideas with colleagues works better or, conversely, that your best ideas come from a sudden burst of inspiration. Innovation, just like leadership, is a very subjective and personal quality. My advice is to keep tinkering and looking around. Continuing education is a great place for experimentation, trial and error, and, of course, success.

Innovation Checklist

1. Description of idea/innovation.

2. Anticipated outcome of implementation.

3. Has idea been implemented elsewhere? How familiar are you with outcomes?

4. Resources required (people, equipment, cash).

5. Ease of implementation, including time required.

6. Criteria for evaluating success of innovation.

7. Period required to determine if successful.

8. Permissions required and from whom.

9. Additional comments.

Perseverance, Motivation, and the Ability to Compromise

Of all the essential leadership traits in higher education, perseverance ranks at the top. Despite what some people (mostly faculty) would have you believe, it is not just a game of intelligence. We are all roughly comparable in our intelligence or we wouldn't be in higher education. And, as we also know there are many different types of intelligence (Gardner, 1983); otherwise the arts and humanities faculty couldn't share the same campus with the science folks, not to mention with engineers and accountants. Sniping about intelligence is just one of those silly things about university life.

My first lesson in perseverance occurred early in my Stony Brook career. Coming from the Smithsonian, where our modest salaries were benchmarked against government pay scales, I had no idea how high university salaries actually were. I figured that my pay was very good, since it was substantially above what I was being paid in D.C. But after a few months on campus I had heard talk about what others were making. The faculty union maintained a list of all salaries and it was easy for me to verify the shocking truth. My pay was toward the bottom of what other deans were earning.

I contacted the provost to see if my situation could be improved. This was easier said than done. Not because he was evasive...he was anything but that. It was due to his prodigious energy level. The man was simply amazing. Often I would meet with him at 8 a.m. and I could swear he was already on his third or fourth meeting while I was still waking up! He was the kind of person who could never waste a minute. Since I too am always multitasking, this made us kindred spirits of a sort. But I was far from being in his league. His high energy level made him a great leader in that he was always encouraging me to try something new and work harder. He also had a great sense of humor. One of his best lines was delivered in front of the faculty, when he stepped down as provost, declaiming that his departure was due to "illness and exhaustion"–the president was "sick and tired" of him! Later I came to realize how tenuous the relationship between provosts and presidents could be.

I could never seem to pin the provost down to talk about money. In all fairness it was a predicament of my own making since at our second interview held to tie down the loose ends of my appointment he asked what salary I expected and was it for "9 months or 12?" Because I always worked year round, like everyone else at the Smithsonian, I said "12." I should have suspected that his quick "OK" meant I had chosen wrongly. I also didn't realize that a dean's salary is customarily computed as an additional 20% beyond nine month's base pay. This is what comes from not knowing the appropriate ground rules. Now I see how long it takes candidates take to work out all the aspects of their employment including spousal/significant other hiring and tenure.

Back to rectifying my own salary problem, I relentlessly stalked an evasive provost. I knew he worked in his office on weekends so I called him at home Saturday evening and asked if he planned on being in Sunday morning. He said, "Yes, but don't come to see me if it's about money!" Thus ended our brief conversation. Well, there was no way for me to back down. I showed up, we talked, and a modest raise came my way. Not as much as I wanted, but enough to justify the effort. There were several good lessons embedded in this episode which would be reinforced many times again in the future.

First, pursue your quarry no matter where it takes you. And no matter how many times you have to ask. Some university students intrinsically grasp this principle and pester us until we finally give in. I have a maxim that you must request everything at least three times. And then a fourth! People are so busy, the resources stretched so thin, the demands so incessant, it is impossible to flag people down, much less obtain the response you desire. So, whenever you request something that is not readily forthcoming, the recipient of your appeal performs a mental "triage," trying to assess your degree of desperation. If "minor" to "moderate," you haven't got a chance. Also, under any circumstances, crying always beats yelling. But you can't overdo or attempt to apply the same strategy over and over again.

Lesson two, there is a lot of bluffing going around, and you have to be willing to call it and dig in your heels when the situation requires this gamble. Bear in mind that very often the people you will meet at the senior levels of college administration have had somewhat charmed and narrow lives, and now they are deferred to on a regular basis. They've gone from professor to chair to dean; a seamless flow of success and honor. Also, for the most part, they've only dealt with faculty like themselves, often drawn from the same narrow disciplines. What do they know about continuing education? My experience with five provosts and a score of deans is that they know very little. If they came from other schools, what they are familiar with is not necessarily what takes place within your bureau. Remember, you need to educate. Also the headiness of recently acquired high office can lead them to magisterial flights of fancy, omniscience, and control.

Stand your ground. Be forceful. Three provosts have thrown me out of their offices, and I'm sure the others have wanted to. And I have also stalked out. In the heat of argument I'll admit to crossing the line of decorum. This only proves, in my mind at least, that I care strongly about the issues. Also, when it's one-on-one there is much more behavioral latitude than when a group is present. You should never allow yourself to be intimidated by superior numbers. On occasion I've brought an overwhelming force to a meeting when I suspected that this strategy would be employed against me! On the other hand, know when it's time to fold your cards and leave the table. You don't want to be known as a sore loser or, much worse, a whiner.

My third lesson is in compromise. I'm not sure where I read this, but the gist of it is that if you can't get a full meal, settle for a sandwich. My refinement of this aphorism is sometimes you have to settle for a pickle! Still, it is an incremental improvement, and you are better off having it than not. Where you decide to draw the line is a very personal thing. I know some people who won't give an inch and others who are too timid to bring up issues that they know others will resist. What it boils down to is that you have to live with yourself. I've found that compromise works. After this incident I ended up reading quite a bit about how to negotiate. Some of these books were more scholarly and research-based. Others were written for a general audience. Invariably I found the latter more insightful and useful. For an example, see Schatzki (1981).

A valuable point to keep in mind, when you are on the other side of the table and have more leverage than your adversaries, is to give in a little. This way you minimize resentment and their desire for getting even. In universities people rarely leave the playing field until they die or retire, whichever comes first. Moreover, a professor may become a chair, dean, provost, or the reverse. I've been at Stony Brook for 18 years and have repeatedly seen this happen. If you are playing for the long haul (and I hope you are) it's important to leave people their dignity and some cash too when possible. If you get a reputation as a bastard (you will rarely come across one in continuing education) your days will be short and not necessarily sweet. Ask yourself, how you would feel about someone who always left you the short end of the stick? It is not Machiavelli, but more like the Godfather. You do a favor and get to ask a favor somewhere down the road. And vice-versa.

I think by nature I am a compromiser, so trying to strike the right balance is important to me. Although as I get older, I can detect a growing tendency to take a harder line. I'm not quite sure why this is. Maybe I'm afraid that I've given up too much over the years and could have done better for my school. Or perhaps it is overconfidence in being, at least for now, an experienced survivor. At any rate, I don't think this is the right way to get what you need, and will be watching myself more closely, checking for any excessive hubris. You have to know when enough is too much.

Within the past few years a number of faculty members with whom I have had close and friendly ties have migrated to senior administrative positions. While I can't assume that they will see everything from my perspective, I can at least be fairly certain that there are no axes to grind. And if we should seriously disagree, I've got to remember to temper my responses accordingly. After all, I'm lucky that they are familiar with continuing education and respect the work.

The fourth and perhaps most important lesson is to avoid a black and white view of the campus universe. When everything seems to be going against you and even the person who hired you won't toss you a bone, it's easy to see the world in terms of stark black and white. Especially from what is often the beleaguered foxhole of continuing education. You've got to grab hold of yourself and remember why you took this job and, even more, why they hired you. It was to perform good works and to be effective. If you think of the promises that were made to you initially as simply statements of positive intent you are less likely to feel betrayed, cheated, or misled in matters of budgeting, staffing, and so forth. It is simply a very competitive world with insufficient resources. You've got to do the best you can with what you have. Often it is settling for a "minimally satisfactory" versus an "optimal" solution. The difference being that in the case of the former, you can get the job done, but at a level less than what is really required.

And last, but not least, prior to negotiating contract terms, learn as much about the new terrain as you possibly can. In your position, what can you reasonably expect? There will be some guesswork involved, and you may have to directly ask, "What is the salary range among deans?" What is the sabbatical policy? Why risk a guess, or make assumptions, when so much is at stake?

Some Final Words on Salary

I don't know of anyone who is happy with his or her salary. Everyone feels entitled to more and can usually identify someone else on campus doing the same or similar job, but with significantly higher compensation. If their salary is among the very highest, they will use as a comparison other institutions or occupations where people are better paid. So, if you are dissatisfied, welcome to the club.

As a dean or director of continuing education, expect to earn less than almost all of the other academic deans at your school. This is true nationally and is reflected in the

annual *Chronicle of Higher Education* (2004) surveys of administrators. Data gathered by the University Continuing
Education Association (UCEA) show a correlation between
the deans' or directors' salaries and institutional size. And
there are some colleges and universities that are just
wealthier and pay more across the board. Depending on
the institution, raises for administrators may be less frequent than for faculty, the assumption being that we are
overpaid to begin with.

How important is salary to your job satisfaction? If it's
one factor among many, join the legion of gripers who nonetheless are able to stay productive in their jobs. Yes, I will
admit to feeling at times unappreciated and undervalued,
but this is a common campus ailment, not unique to continuing education. There are some people who see salary
as a way of keeping score, as indicative of how well they are
doing. If you conflate your worth to this single measure you
will be making a *terrible mistake* and robbing yourself of
the satisfaction that comes from savoring a job well done.

On Reputation and Decision Making

There is a scene (Act II, Scene iii) in Shakespeare's
Othello, where Cassio, "the honorable lieutenant," is duped
by the evil Iago and totally humiliated, losing face and position. In desperation he declaims, "Reputation, reputation,
reputation! O, I have lost my reputation! I have lost the
immortal part of myself, and what remains is bestial."
We've seen it ourselves in politics and throughout public
life when someone whom we admire and respect is brought
down by a single, thoughtless, but well-publicized act. A life-
time of accomplishment is seemingly erased by the dispro-
portionate attention paid to an error in judgment, a case of
foot in mouth disease, or just being in the wrong place at
the wrong time.

I've repeated Cassio's lines to my family, especially to
my children, Shari and Avi, numerous times and now it is
something of a family joke. But to me the message is seri-

ous, indeed. You live and die by your reputation. And what is exceedingly difficult to achieve is easily lost. I know it shouldn't be so, but it is. The university is no different, in this respect. It can be, like any large organization, equally vicious. I'm not by any means recommending a rigid self-censorship. In any case it would never work since so much of what we do is spontaneous, seat-of-the-pants decision making where we interact with others on the fly, as we rush from one meeting or engagement to the next, in the parking lot, crossing the quad, or in the hallways. You simply can't attempt to script these and I even think it is good for people to catch glimpses of your unguarded inner self. Let them know what they're dealing with.

Regarding Cassio, my message is really quite different. It is to be aware that there are consequences for every action...and in choosing one course of action over another we are inviting the likelihood of one set of outcomes instead of others. The prior sentence, couched in so much ambiguity, is just about useless as a guide to action. The future, as we all know, is unpredictable, despite how carefully we hedge our bets. Perhaps an analogy would be to the Middle Ages when people were exhorted to memento mori, to be mindful of death as the inescapable reality of everyday life, lurking around every corner, waiting to snatch the living for an untimely demise. Instead I propose memento consequenti. Assess, act, reassess. And if necessary, redress. If you've made a decision and something is still bothering you, maybe you need to fine-tune a little.

I am a firm believer in active, real-time, frequent decision making, even before all the data are in. If I think my judgment has been flawed or that my emotion has gotten the better of me, I apologize. If I propose something that later seems unfair, I'll revisit the subject. Or if I've been short or rushed with someone, the next time I see that person, I try to make it up. The great thing about our jobs is that we have multiple opportunities to set things right. We have phone, fax, email, correspondence, as well as more personal encounters to reach out and refine our dealings. Especially on a campus, where people are in day-to-day contact, there should be no reason for letting a poor decision or action simply run its course. Make a quick U turn and get back on track!

Becoming an Effective Leader

The most important thing you have to remember is that there is a broad range of acceptable leadership behavior. Somewhere between complete laissez-faire and repressive totalitarianism there is plenty of space for us to operate. At the first session of my leadership workshops and courses I bring in a sack of books. They can range from *The Tao of Leadership* (Heider, 1988) , *Leadership Secrets of Attila the Hun* (Roberts, 1987), *Jesus CEO* (Jones, 1995) *The Nursing Father: Moses as a Political Leader* (Wildavsky, 1984), *The Charismatic Leader* (Conger, 1989), *Leading with Soul* (Bolman & Deal, 1995), and *Primal Leadership* (Goleman, Boyatzis & McKee, 2002) in order to suggest the variety of titles, popular and semi-academic. My course texts, in contrast, are research-based. Bass, (1990) is one example and not as much fun to read as the popular literature. Because of inconclusive research findings that are often contradicted in other reports, students are dismayed when they discover that there is an absence of scientific certitude as to which type of leadership is actually "best." This, of course, is the liberating moment I love, when they realize that they won't find the answer in a book, or even in a score of studies.

My philosophy is that only through a combination of reading, study, and self-critical reflection, all in an ongoing cycle, will we be able to improve. It takes commitment, the ability to acknowledge mistakes and, not surprisingly, continuing education for this to happen. Very often the popular literature, including autobiographies, is of more value than detached scholarly analysis. Students are able to identify with the author and experience vicariously the situations and the actions taken. Honest authors will also address failure and how they bounced back. This resilience in the face of adversity is critical to success in continuing education. If a book recounts only triumph after triumph, it's a safe bet that the author is holding back. Maybe it is my own sense of struggle, but I prefer reading about others who have a history of repeatedly surmounting obstacles.

I realize this may be a cultural bias, maybe even familial. My father was an immigrant and my mother a first generation American. Growing up, the importance of constant effort as a lifestyle was driven home. I was taught that nothing could be taken for granted and to be passive in life was to invite disaster. So I grew up always looking over my shoulder, trying to be prepared for no matter what might be ahead. I approached the study of leadership as a survival skill that had to be mastered. And my subsequent writing and teaching on that subject are simply other ways of honing my expertise and learning from others.

In the realm of leadership, no one can have the final word since for each of us it is different, and there are always new circumstances and individuals with which to contend. One of the things I do is to try to see my actions from the perspective of others. I ask how I would react were the situation reversed? There are probably many limitations to this approach, but I have found it very helpful in developing a course of action, and then, later, a cycle of review. You might think that this is a lot of wasted effort. But I can't think of another way for myself. Admittedly I am working within the context of my own personality and upbringing, hence my disclaimer at the outset that no single size fits all. I encourage you to experiment with different approaches until you find a way that is right for you.

It's also important to remember that it is not just a matter of intellect, otherwise all smart people would be great leaders, and any quick check of your campus will quickly refute that erroneous assumption. I remember an observation attributed to the late Nobel laureate George Wald, to the effect that he would rather be ruled by the first 50 people listed in the Boston phone book than a like number drawn from the Harvard faculty! This is a tough pill for some deans and provosts to swallow. But the best among them will learn that it is more than a matter of intellectual smarts. *Primal*

Leadership by Daniel Goleman et al. (2002) speaks to this issue. And the entire corpus of writings on charismatic leadership also attests to how great leaders have reached beyond logic and reasoning to connect and inspire others.

More problematic than leadership is the issue of followership. When I bring this up for discussion among my students it is hard to generate any great enthusiasm. It seems that we all want to get out there and lead. This is especially true with the drive to move ahead in administration, where greater leadership responsibility is regarded as the hallmark of success. Yet, if I am at all honest, this is where I fall short in my own estimation. I can't follow. Or, I don't want to. It is so hard for me to go along and buy into others' decisions and plans. As a consequence, I leave plenty of decision-making slack for SPD staff because I refuse to be hypocritical. I'm open to discussion, debate, and disagreement in thought as well as in deed. It doesn't mean I will necessarily change my mind but I will certainly listen. The leaders I respect most will afford me the same courtesy. Thankfully I work in a university community where people are paid to think differently.

Keep in mind that most people in your department will automatically defer to you because of your rank and title. Don't ever mistake this for genuine agreement; they are just backing off because of your positional authority. Fear in the workplace can *never* be entirely eliminated, regardless of how fair and democratic you may be. We have all seen and experienced the naked exercise of misused power and are all aware that it could easily be directed against us. Which brings me to another point: As dean or director you are expected to exercise authority in order to achieve important institutional goals. If, for some reason, you have deep philosophical reasons for not wishing to direct the behavior of others, then moving up in the administrative hierarchy is probably not for you. I find I am always tinkering with my school, moving things around, starting new projects, shifting duties from one person to another for the sake of improvement. I try to be as respectful of others as possible, but I would never refuse to act because of the anticipated negative reaction of others.

The classic dilemma in leadership is to strike the right balance between institutional and personal goals for yourself and others. Metaphorically speaking, in terms of extremes, it can't be either a "country club" or a "chain gang." We've got to produce by whatever standards are established for continuing education within our respective environments. How do we reconcile respect for others and achieving a good bottom line? This is one of those questions that is far easier to raise and answer in the abstract than in the fluid day-to-day world of work.

Because of the fundamental collegial ethos of higher education, treating people poorly will not burnish your reputation. Quite the opposite—you will be undermining yourself. The university is a glass house with almost complete transparency. So above all, treat your staff well especially if your standards are high. You'd be surprised how many people wish to work hard to achieve important goals. In fact, the more important the goals, the harder people will work. Your job is to identify important goals and stimulate a coordinated group effort in their achievement.

A key idea I wish to share is my conviction that all work is *volunteered*, especially in the quest of excellence. I see my staff as volunteering to help me. The minute I believe they are *required* to perform as I wish, I have made a terrible mistake. Excellence can never be coerced. The same for innovation. Superior performance, because it requires extra effort, can only come about through the *willingness* of others. The only performance you can coerce is at the minimal threshold of acceptability. Think about all those other places, on campus and off, where people seem to be just going through the motions. I'm willing to bet it is because leadership has stopped trying to motivate and inspire and is just settling for what is deemed acceptable. To have the best office of continuing education you have to inspire others to strive toward their own ideals of excellence. And since they know their jobs better than you, it is only through their efforts and understanding that this goal will be accomplished. Leadership is hard work. I'm still trying to improve after more than 30 years. I have much to learn.

The Use of Power

After decision making, the second most difficult area for prospective deans and directors is in the exercise of power. Like everything else I've said, this too becomes an issue of fitting your behavior to your own sense of values and personality; no single correct formula exists. Those qualifications aside, I offer some observations on power and its application.

Our field of continuing education, with its liberal, egalitarian culture, has a difficult time with power. This probably stems from our work with adult students who are often our peers in terms of age, responsibilities, education, and social class. Add to this a campus academic environment of independence and collegiality—if not outright hostility to authority—and you are left with a milieu where the exercise of power is questionable at best. Although administrative areas more easily embrace standard workplace hierarchies of authority, continuing education's outright espousal of teamwork also acts as a leavening agent. Therefore power, in any of its guises, must be applied sparingly and with discretion.

Why is power necessary? It might be argued that continuing education professionals know what to do, and that deans and directors need to simply provide adequate resources and then just step aside, occasionally pointing out opportunities, or drawing attention to new projects. This laissez-faire approach takes too much for granted and is erected on the flimsy foundation of wishful thinking. I know there are people who subscribe to this approach, but they rarely become deans of continuing education—they become college presidents.

The clearest approach to this topic may be considered a little indelicate, but I can't think of a way around it: How do you feel about telling other people what to do? This, in essence, is getting to the heart of the subject. How you go about doing it is another matter. Being able to actively influence the duties and behavior of others is what power is about. You take it upon yourself to determine what members of your staff should be doing, intervening when necessary. You may have a pleasant office environment, but it is definitely not a rest home. I know of colleagues who have left the deanship because of a frustration borne of not being able to direct staff and being unhappy with the disappointing consequences.

There are plenty of good books that look at power. My favorite for an overall treatment is *Bass & Stogdill's Handbook of Leadership* (1990). In some areas it may now be dated, but the comprehensive, research-based analysis in this 10-pound volume still can't be matched. The book presents a nuanced picture that defies any ironclad conclusions. So why do I value their treatment? Because it realistically reflects the confusing world I inhabit with all of its complications, complexities, and conundrums. Each day I tiptoe through emotional minefields of personalities, rethinking and recalibrating my strategies. It's possible that I'm not a good model for you. I can't give you a perfect formulation; I don't even have one myself. I push very hard to get my way— directly, obliquely, sometimes through understatement and misdirection. In my case, Emerson's observation that "an institution is the lengthened shadow of one man" may well be true (cited in Bartlett, 1992, p. 431). I embrace the power that comes with my position; I couldn't hope to live up to my responsibilities without it.

Personal Work Styles

You're going to be judged by the quality and quantity of your work, how you treat other people, and your overall value to the campus. Just being in your office, putting in your time, doesn't cut it. And forget about impressing people with your long hours, short lunches, the many times your face appears in the local newspapers, and the few (if any) vacations. What counts is your effectiveness, which will rightfully be assessed by the substance of your accomplishments. Thus it is vitally important to develop a personal work style that engenders success. Here are some of the things that work for me.

I keep my own calendar and schedule my own appointments and lunches including most multi-party meetings. I also answer my own phone. I could easily have someone else do all this; in fact I once did, but found I was wasting too much time, my most valuable resource, in going back and forth with my assistants. I meet with whom I want when I want. Sometimes instead of a meeting I'll make a phone call or schedule a lunch or a breakfast or a coffee break. I have to eat and I drink a lot of coffee. Sometimes an email will suffice. I want to have blocks of uninterrupted time to tackle the most important projects. By handling my appointments I can achieve this efficiently. Mintzberg's (1973) characterization of managerial life as *brief, varied*, and *fragmented* is all too true. He based his findings upon hundreds of hours of structured observation discovering that managers were always being distracted and interrupted, unable to focus on a single problem for more than a few minutes before another clamored for attention. By handling my own time, I can often avoid this predicament. Remember: the trappings of having an assistant can be a trap.

For phone calls, if I am busy I'll let phone mail take it. Otherwise I'll answer it myself. If I can't help the caller, I make a referral to someone else on staff. Caller ID lets me know who's on the line, and I have the flexibility again of taking the call or responding to it later. People are impressed when the dean is answering his own phone. Sometimes a caller will ask why I do it and I say it's easier for me. And it's true. Many times, in response to a letter, I will make a call instead of writing. People value the quick response, and once again are pleased that I am handling this personally. A call also saves me time, especially when it is a difficult issue and I would have to labor over a complicated response to a convoluted problem. I have to admit, too, that there are some calls I never return. And there are also some that I shouldn't take but do. Just recently I accepted a call from a part-time instructor who needed a computer and projector for his evening course. I was curious about the current procedure, so I followed up myself, and then reported to him.

If a meeting is an absolute must, I have a number of strategies. The obvious one is to state at the outset how much time I have so the visitor is encouraged to quickly get to the point. In other cases, when the meeting is impromptu but unavoidable, I will meet in my reception area, which although comfortable, tends to set limitations on the discussion. If it turns out to be something requiring privacy, we can then go to my office. If I am meeting with someone on a subject that I intuit that I will subsequently refer to someone else on the staff for action, I have the meeting in that person's office so I can leave after a few minutes. This same rationale leads me to include colleagues in deliberations earlier rather than later.

I know many people are unable to delegate because they want it done "just so" but that's not me. I accept that others will do it differently, and quickly hand off an assignment if I believe someone else has the expertise or if it is more appropriate for them by virtue of rank and responsibilities. Maybe we will talk about it or maybe I will say "just handle it and let me know how it turns out." I estimate that more than 70% of my time is spent meeting and talking with staff. I'll drop in for updates or invite people down for a chat. I try to be very accessible. And when I am with a staff member I always close the door, even for a brief or seemingly inconsequential matter. That way I can give undivided attention for as long as necessary. In my mind this is a mark of respect to the people who work with me.

I try to be very clear about my expectations. Typically, on collaborative projects I strive for a quick turnaround, trying to move to closure without unnecessary delay. I'm also a quick decision-maker so as not to hold others back who are waiting on my response. You have to know the difference between $20, $20,000 or $200,000 decisions and act accordingly. I try not to get bogged down in minutiae and save that level of analysis for when it is really necessary. Then I take out the microscope, fine-toothed comb, or whatever, and have at it.

My memos/emails are short and to the point. Very often it's just "see me." Although I write a great deal, I have greater trust in my ability to communicate sensitive topics verbally and feel that important matters are best discussed personally. I consider myself a "hands-on" manager with a fair knowledge of everything that goes on in a very complicated school. I have strong opinions but will avoid at all costs trying to come off as a know-it-all. I dislike people like that. Who doesn't?

Well-run universities are decentralized. I'm comfortable in this kind of environment and basically want to be left alone to run SPD. Effective deans need to have this confidence in themselves, and hopefully it proves justified. Is there a contradiction here since I always feel free to intervene with other staff when I believe it to be required? I don't think so, since my responsibility for the entire school must outweigh how individuals may feel in every instance. I'm open to give and take, but reserve final decision-making authority and won't hesitate to reassign staff, add new duties, or eliminate old ones in the interests of SPD's academic effectiveness. It's impossible for me to stand by and not take action; it's my temperament and style.

Here's another tip that will help improve both intra-office communication and morale: the round robin. At our regular staff meetings we go around the room and all staff members are expected to contribute. This can be as little as "I'm very busy" to a recap of a major success, or a description of a brand new initiative. With 30 people, it takes about a half hour, at the minimum. But it is a great way for everyone to catch up on what's going on, share a laugh, or jointly focus on a problem. You'd be surprised at the things that come up requiring attention, but that otherwise would not be shared. I believe this practice is also ennobling to others since it clearly signals that I am interested in what everyone is doing. Sometimes when I am sitting at someone else's meeting I wish there would be a round robin. I want to hear what my fellow deans are up to and this would give me a chance to share as well. Why is there such resistance to incorporating this worthwhile and easy-to-implement idea? Does it mean that people don't really want to listen to others? I'm afraid that this is too often true.

Leadership Succession and Success

Rarely, if ever, have I heard leadership succession discussed, unless it is to commiserate with a colleague who was not promoted to the top continuing education slot at his or her school. That is because it is rare, when a vacancy occurs at the senior level, to recruit from within, except for someone stepping up in a temporary acting capacity, until a new dean or director from outside is recruited. I find it hard to understand the logic of this approach, especially if the departing head has created a well-functioning and successful department. Yet, because hiring an outsider is the well-recognized norm, continuing education administrators must accept the inevitability of relocation and the need for mobility if they aspire to the deanship.

Campus leaders may be seeking a fresh vision and new ideas or planning to reconfigure the university's approach to continuing education. Those currently onboard could be viewed as too tied to the status quo, or just not up to the task. In any case, since succession is tricky and clouded in uncertainty, we give little thought to naming a replacement, since we lack the authority to ensure this individual's appointment. Advancement in continuing education becomes contingent on the availability of external opportunities and the willingness to seek them. A constructive result of this dynamic is the cross-fertilization that occurs when the new dean or director undertakes a major review of existing programs and policies as a prelude to implementing new projects and plans.

Research I conducted on predicting the successful changeover of new continuing education directors (1989b) identified a number of different possible approaches to the transition process. Interestingly, all of the directors in the study, successful or not, anticipated making career changes in a few years that would take them <u>out</u> of continuing education. This was surprising and raised questions about the long term rewards anticipated by members of our profession. Future scholarship could examine the interaction of personality and institutional characteristics, and how this contributes to effective long-term service. This would be both interesting and valuable.

Lessons Learned

It is one of the inescapable features of organizational life that even though we lead others, we are in turn led. When I look back over the years I can easily identify my good and bad supervisors. The former treated me with respect and encouraged me to innovate. It was just the opposite for those I considered poor. Most people I reported to were somewhere in the middle, oscillating from one end of the continuum to the other, depending on issue or maybe even day of the week. Ignoring my feelings for a moment, who's to say which approach worked best in getting the most out of me—the nurturing father or Darth Vader?

We develop our leadership strategies based upon the situations and people we face and, if lucky, somehow manage to get by and succeed. One thing I've noticed is that poor leaders cause their followers to express considerable worry and doubt, thereby undermining performance. When these staff members speak among themselves and commiserate, the morale of the entire department is at risk. Because campus environments are transparent, this dissatisfaction will eventually get out beyond your division causing others to doubt your competence. Try not to be a scold. Instead discover opportunities to reinforce cohesion and teamwork. Even if you are conservative by nature try to expand your comfort zone to tolerate a greater degree of risk-taking. It's essential for continued growth.

CHAPTER 8

Discovering the World of Continuing Education

Developing an Identity As a "Professional"

At the Smithsonian my job was rather one-dimensional as a program developer/manager. By way of contrast, at Stony Brook many doors were simultaneously open. Beyond creating, scheduling, and managing curricula, the campus environment encouraged a much broader range of creative intellectual activity including research, writing, teaching, and all forms of interdepartmental relationships. In other words, beyond working as hard as I wanted, I could also diversify my skills, adding variety and depth to my role as the compleat continuing educator.

In my mind I already had a captivating image of what I thought campus life should be. It involved quiet contemplation of great issues amidst the swirl of aromatic tobacco, the discussion of same with other tweed-jacketed colleagues, afternoons of sherry receptions at the faculty club as a means of recuperation from the day's toil, teaching the occasional course attended by young acolytes, and evenings of chamber music at the campus Fine Arts Center. The reality was beyond my expectations. First, the great ideas had to do with increasing enrollment; the campus was a no-smoking zone; faculty rarely wore sport coats or suits; there was no faculty club; my classes were late in the evening and very fatiguing; and when I finally arrived home after a long, hard day, I was so exhausted, the mere thought of returning to campus, even for some relaxing chamber music, was a non-starter. So much for my illusions. Still, it was and continues to be a very stimulating environment. Everyone I met had

either a book in press or was working on a new one, or they
were writing articles, giving papers, traveling all over the
world, and obviously having a great time. So how was I to
begin?

I had published a little over the years. The first was an
article, based upon my City Tech experiences, on forming a
continuing education alumni chapter. There were also one
or two reports I presented at conferences, but not much
more. Frankly, I was just too busy with program development to even think about contributions to the literature.
And there was another very good reason too. As I recounted
earlier, my entry into the field of continuing education was
by accident. It was not as if I had deliberately directed myself towards this career. I needed a job and the position of
Evening Administrator was available.

In all of my coursework at NYU there was no mention of
adult education or of any relevant literature. But, because
City Tech was affiliated with what was then called the Adult
Education Association of the USA (AEA/USA) I began to
receive the newsletter *Adult Leadership,* where my first
article appeared (Edelson, 1976). The AEA/USA sought to
unify within a single professional organization the entire
range of adult education practice and thus bring coherence
to a field that had been traditionally fractured by institutional setting. Colleges and universities, community and
junior colleges, public school adult education, and other
state and community providers all had their own separate
organizations. An example is the now-defunct National Association of Public School Adult Educators (NAPSAE) which
was very influential in the 1950s and 1960s.

Because the AEA/USA sought to minister to adult education at-large, its publications were very general, and
tended to address facets of the continuing education skill-
set that would be of value regardless of setting. So they
published articles on leadership, marketing, administration,
and so forth. Because of my evening work hours, and the
lack of anyone to back me up, I was unable to attend any of
their conferences or meetings. In all of my four years of
NYCCC I can honestly say that my knowledge of continu-

ing education was limited to on-the-job training and a little reading. This was to change at the Smithsonian where I was more thoroughly socialized into the profession.

The Smithsonian Resident Associate Program held a membership in the National University Extension Association (NUEA), the forerunner of today's University Continuing Education Association (UCEA). Incidentally, one of the many items of interest I was to learn about organized continuing education was the frequent name changes of organizations. For example, the NUEA, before morphing into the UCEA, was for a time the NUCEA, the National University Continuing Education Association. The AEA/USA, originally founded as the Adult Education Association, became the American Association for Adult Education (AAAE), and still later, the AAACE (American Association for Adult and Continuing Education). Another major organization, the Association for Continuing Higher Education (ACHE), had been founded as the Association of University Evening Colleges (AUEC).

These name changes, far from being frivolous, reflect the evolving self-identity of continuing education practitioners and their perceptions of the field. Lately, among colleges and universities, there has been a marked trend in the nomenclature away from Schools and Divisions of Continuing Education and the substitution of the terms Professional Studies or Professional Development.

At the Smithsonian I was encouraged to become involved in the NUEA and soon found myself regularly attending and speaking at regional and national meetings. One of things that struck me as unusual about these gatherings was their openness and receptivity to new participants. Perhaps the beleaguered nature of the field meant that new members were especially welcome. Or that continuing education's reliance upon new ideas placed a premium upon young, bright minds that could infuse the organization with innovation. Most people were too busy to read unless it was about marketing; and even fewer published.

The egalitarian nature of the UCEA made it possible for me to become active in the organization at both the local

and national levels. I was a regular participant in continuing education conferences and workshops, was elected Chair
of the Mid-Atlantic Region, and served on the National
Board of Directors. Networking relationships with other
professionals became a key benefit of my membership. I
could always call on someone else when faced with a difficult challenge, or when I needed a shoulder to lean on.

My dilemma in confronting a desire to publish was that
I didn't know the literature of my newly chosen career.
Learning about the existence of doctoral programs in adult
education prompted me to attend the conferences of the
Commission of Professors of Adult Education (CPAE), the
faculty association for those in academic Departments of
Adult Education where these graduate programs were often situated. To my knowledge, I was the only dean at the
CPAE meetings. I learned that I was a practitioner as opposed to an academic. In contrast with the capitalistic world
inhabited by deans and directors, CPAE members reside in
an ideological realm, removed from the nitty-gritty of budgets, enrollment targets, and the incessant competition for
resources.

Some professors who are teaching in adult education
doctoral programs are themselves located in departments
with a somewhat broader orientation such as human development, human resource management, educational administration and leadership, or higher education. This reflects
the applied nature of our field and its connections with other
areas of education and management. And although these
adult education graduate courses and degrees are certainly
more plentiful than when I attended graduate school, en-
trance to the field is still from so many different directions,
defying any simple classification.

Within the past few years I've noticed that some organizations in continuing education, especially the Association
for Continuing Higher Education (ACHE) and the Commission of Professors, maintain very active online discussions
among their members. Frequently someone in one of these
organizations, will ask about some new type of program they
are curious about, or a tuition or funding policy, and re-

ceive more than a score of helpful responses. I coined a term to describe this phenomenon: "just-in-time colleagues" since very often the respondents do not even know each other beforehand. What a contrast to when we had long-established networks built up over years of conferencing. Today's world of continuing education has so many new participants cycling in and out that this form of instant collegiality makes more sense than having to rely solely upon people you met at a conference. Just think—if I wanted to learn about organizing continuing education programs in community libraries, I could sample the ACHE membership in as much time as it takes to type this sentence. It would be a good place to begin my research.

Continuing Education and the Campus

At one point, in the 1980s it appeared that the prevailing mode of campus organization for continuing education would remain large, centralized bureaus in effect, the adult education provider for the entire campus through which other schools, departments and divisions of the college would deploy their outreach programs (see Edelson, 1995). Continuing education's expertise, in this campus division of labor, would be to assist in developing, marketing, and administering the programs. There would also be a sharing of revenue between continuing education and its clients in the academic sector.

Schools that arranged their continuing education organizations in this centralized manner often grew quite large with staff in the hundreds at some campuses. Internally the organization of the unit might have demarcations between credit and noncredit, each with an assistant or associate dean. And within these subdivisions program directors were responsible, as I was at the Smithsonian, for course and workshop development. The administrative core would have budget and marketing specialists, a human resource division—in short all the trappings of a separate college. Some of the continuing education divisions were in fact referred to as "University Colleges" and in one case, the University of Maryland University College is indeed a free-standing institution, separately accredited, with its own president. More frequently, the chief continuing education academic administrator is either a dean or director.

With the field rationally organized as I have just described, it was possible for me to visualize a career path, although much attenuated, progressing from program coordinator to dean. In the 1990s this arrangement fractured as collegiate continuing education was decentralized. Impetus for these changes was provided by a national recession which, in the case of many state universities, resulted in declining allocations for higher education, compelling schools to raise tuition and to pay greater attention to supplementary income streams including continuing education. In the case of private universities, declining endowment revenue based upon a depressed stock market produced similar outcomes.

As cost savings measures, centralized continuing education offices were closed and their programs shifted. Organizational nodes were now dispersed throughout the university, each school or college running its own programs and retaining all revenues generated. New heads of continuing education within the various colleges were more likely to have come out of those fields, for example engineering or business, rather than having a background in continuing education per se. As a consequence, the coherence and professional identity of continuing education as a whole have diminished. Yet the need for a continuing education skill-set among these practitioners still obtains.

The field continues to evolve. The ubiquity of continuing education as a feature of higher education, in all types and sizes of institutions and in nearly all divisions, is accelerating the drive toward greater specialization. This will mitigate direct competition between and within schools as every director searches out a unique niche. At my own campus, for example, another office has decided to offer corporate training. Historically this has been an SPD activity, but on a small scale. Rather than two areas contesting for a diminutive audience, we have moved away from this function to an outreach area that is much more fecund and where we can expand without competition.

Because the need for continuing and adult education will grow unabated, along with the complexity of the American economy, there will be no shortage of new program possibilities or of students. Looking back 30 years, I can now see that I entered adult education as it was beginning to evolve into a mainstreamed dimension of higher education, with many more options and opportunities for students and professionals. But at the time, particularly as I moved from City Tech to the Smithsonian, and then to Stony Brook I had no perspective or grasp of continuing education beyond the focus of my own institutions and their distinct priorities for adult learning. Like the sailboat, I found myself pushed in one way and then another, depending upon where I was working. I required greater insight into adult and continuing education and turned to scholarship and teaching as a way of understanding myself within this dynamic and unpredictable career.

Scholarly Strivings

Professor Robert Boice headed Stony Brook's first Teaching Performance Center (TPC) which had been established in the early 1990s as a bureau for improving classroom instruction. Since that time the office has been rechristened as the Center for Excellence in Learning and Teaching (CELT), but the mission remains the same: to enhance quality teaching, especially in the undergraduate classroom. Why a research university would need an office like this is abundantly clear to anyone who has ever worked on a campus like ours: teaching historically played second fiddle to research. Fortunately this is now changing.

Professor Boice was a member of the Psychology Department who studied the subject of faculty research and scholarly productivity. He specialized in helping faculty overcome self-imposed barriers to publishing, aka writer's block. He was also an expert at developing and interpreting student assessments of classroom teaching, so he was a perfect choice to head the newly formed TPC. Until I met Bob I had published very little and was unsure of how to go about it. But I felt committed to making a strong effort and sought him out for guidance. Together we reviewed the literature of continuing education, paying special attention to the various journals and the types of articles that regularly appeared. Although this may seem like an exercise in Common Sense 101, it had never before occurred to me to approach writing for publication in this deliberate and methodical way.

Within a short period of time I was writing on whatever aspects of my job seemed interesting or unusually complicated. I learned from Bob that writing for publication was just another skill to be mastered, not the mystery I had made it out to be. Bob believed that just about anyone could be a successful author and looking at my own success, I have to agree. Fortunately I had a generous mentor who helped me overcome my initial insecurity and shared his know-how. I've tried to do the same with others and have coedited a book (Edelson & Malone, 1999) and coauthored a monograph (Edelson, O'Brien, & Brennan 1997) with SPD colleagues who had never before published.

I also consulted history professor Joel Rosenthal for advice on writing books. Another well-regarded teacher/scholar on our campus, Joel's advice was very interesting and although it was at least 15 years ago, I remember it as if it were yesterday. Over lunch at the University Club he advised me to not spend too much time on preparing articles since the prestige value of writing a book far exceeded that of even a bouquet of shorter writings. Moreover, to publish a book you only had to convince usually a single editor, whereas articles in academic journals had to run a gauntlet of very critical colleagues, all more concerned with their own reputations than in helping you to establish your own. I can attest to the frustration of submitting an article, having it rejected, and resubmitting with the recommended changes, only to have it rejected a second time. This is very hard for anyone to take.

Joel also suggested that I make sure to publish at least two books so that people would know that the first wasn't a fluke. And, for the pièce de résistance, I should make sure to publish in a foreign language, a great mark of status and distinction within any university. His advice proved correct. Counting this volume I have five books, one of which was published in German (2000), and one monograph (1997). So I can hold my head high among my academic peers. But as they used to say while I was growing up in Brooklyn, with more than a touch of sarcasm, "that and 15 cents (now $2.00) will get you on the subway." In fact Larry Slobodkin, another Stony Brook colleague, observed that five books is proof of being a hack! Nevertheless, I've enjoyed writing and find that like any skill it improves with practice. I recall a particularly tough time at Stony Brook when writing became my refuge and a place where I could recharge my intellectual and spiritual batteries. And other than teaching, I can't think of a better way to learn about continuing education.

I follow what I call the "rule of three" by identifying multiple outlets for each piece of scholarship: a conference presentation, a published article, and teaching. Because it is difficult for me to find the necessary time to write I have to extract as much value as possible from each unit of output. I share drafts electronically with colleagues at other campuses for their comments, even though I know that most of the time friends are much more generous with their praise than criticism. I value the occasion to exchange viewpoints and sustain collegiality throughout the year. The ability to have new ideas, or to rethink problems from new perspectives, is invaluable. This, I would have to say, is one of the best features of the university environment where intellectual effort is valued and therefore encouraged. Think about it: Stony Brook University must be quite a place if deans can write books.

I assume that there is something to be learned in whatever I am doing and that by writing this lesson is uncovered for me and others. It is important to be liberated from traditional and conventional definitions of administration. I advise you to take advantage of what your own campus has to offer, and to experiment. In addition to my publications I've been invited to speak just about all over the world. I work hard on these talks. As an intellectual bonus, looking at a topic from what I imagine to be the perspective of colleagues in other countries often sheds new light on subjects that interest me, leading to additional writing.

Even with all the writing and speaking you might correctly observe that my impact on the world of continuing education is negligible. What major change or impacts can I identify as an outcome of my activities? All I can claim with certainty is that I've been able to take my belief and dedication to our field and share it with others, motivating them to keep striving towards their own definitions of excellence.

Colleagues, Cultures, and Courses

I think it was several years after coming to Stony Brook when I began to broaden my contacts within the larger field of adult learning. Since I had already worked in an urban community college and a major national museum before joining up with a research university, I was sensitive to the importance of organizational context as a prime determinant of continuing education. Wherever I went, it involved shifting gears, trying to understand the institution's goals and priorities. Despite differences in program content and instructor qualifications I quickly realized that all of us in adult learning, whether teachers, students, or administrators, were members of the same extended family.

I began meeting with continuing education providers based in the public schools, community colleges, business and industry, and in community and nonprofit organizations. I joined the specialized professional organizations representing each sector, read the newsletters, paid the dues. Among the marginal, I was most marginal since I did not quite fit in with the public school people, the human resource department folks, or the state government education types. My perceptions of the world of adult education fit the metaphor of an archipelago: a group of close but separate and distinct islands, each with its own culture and way of doing things, aware of, but not directly concerned with life on the other islands, all of which have evolved differently. Occasionally a person may visit another island but, because it is so different, choose not to live there. There may be a common language, but it is comprised of a multitude of dialects and distinct linguistic conventions. Today it occurred to me that we are also islands within our own institutions.

The more I learned about the different cultures of continuing education the more convinced I became that Stony Brook University could play a useful role in bringing the people of adult education on Long Island together, or at least increasing mutual familiarity. I developed a graduate course, "Principles of Adult Learning," that I taught in the evening as part of the Master of Arts in Liberal Studies (MA/LS) degree. I based the content upon similar courses I had learned about through attending meetings of the CPAE. In addition to lecture/discussion classes I invited guest speakers who represented different sectors of adult education on Long Island. This dimension was fascinating, especially learning how each entered the field. It seemed that most were like me; it was by accident.

The MA/LS degree is very popular among Long Island public school teachers who require a master's in order to obtain their permanent teaching license. In presenting my course to this population I was hoping also to influence the field of public school adult education which has been relatively static as the bulk of the action has shifted to community colleges and universities who are better suited to prepare adults for a changing job market. The course was also an elective in my school's Master of Professional Studies (MPS) Degree, Human Resource Management concentration. This cohort had already made a career commitment to providing adult education in the business sector and my course was for them closer to home professionally.

I tried to cover the most important themes incorporating both foundations of practice as well as an overview of the many domains where adult educators find employment. It was a real challenge to do justice to the field. Imagine, before coming to Stony Brook I had worked for 14 years in continuing education without having studied it. I have since learned that many of my colleagues are in a similar predicament: a combination of on-the-job training, and being too busy to read. Joining the Commission of Professors gave me a jump-start on catching up with the literature, plus I had the motivation of having to teach my course. Within a very short period of time I was able to come up to speed and have even used the same approach with other areas I have needed to learn about quickly. Following the advice of Fred Starr of the Smithsonian's Wilson Center, I promptly read half-dozen recently published books on the subject I wish to learn. The selections can be based on conversations with experts in the field or on books I discover myself. Out of the six initial choices, at least one or two will be particularly helpful; and by using the references cited by those authors I can pursue selected knowledge threads further. I am always acquiring new books on whatever subject currently interests me. You might say I actively take responsibility for my own learning and you'd be correct.

I also created a course on the History of Adult Education in the USA, which I taught Friday nights in the doctoral adult education program at Teachers College, Columbia. This course came about through conversations with Mathias Finger, who was then on the Teacher College faculty. We had met through the CPAE and discovered that we shared a mutual interest in the historical development of adult learning. Mathias was responsible for the AEGIS (Adult Education Guided Intensive Study) Program, a very successful cohort-based doctoral program. The group met for four weekends each semester at the Columbia campus. During the intervening periods they worked independently on assignments. My seminar was held on Friday evenings and was the lead-in to each weekend's program. Students were drawn from all over the United States, including one or two in each group from overseas. Typically a large number had backgrounds in human resource department, several were in university continuing education, the health professions, some in nonprofits; in short, a diverse group coming at adult education from many different angles. I encouraged the students to develop historical perspectives on their particular sector as a way of examining the dynamics of practice and the forces that have shaped it.

In the three or four times I've taught the course I've varied the readings, but the backbone has consisted of Knowles's *A History of the Adult Education Movement in the United States* (1977), Kett's *The Pursuit of Knowledge Under Difficulties* (1994), and Stubblefield and Keane's *Adult Education in the American Experience* (1994). I supplemented these texts with specialized monographs and articles.

Each time during the seminar several students developed publishable articles which subsequently appeared in their professional journals. Overall, I thought the classes went well, although one factor I had to contend with was the lack of academic writing experience among the cohorts. This was at first a shock since they were enrolled in a doctoral program. Later when I experienced the full diversity of the groups, their lack of preparation, though disappointing, was more understandable. Teaching at Teacher College has been beneficial and I am proud to be associated with the AEGIS program and its innovative history.

Both courses were a way of intellectually orienting me to the field, its traditions, and especially its possibilities. I also developed and taught a graduate course on leadership where which improved my own leadership skills, and a master's thesis seminar. Scholarship and teaching have become cornerstones of my own self-knowledge as an adult educator. This is very much in the spirit of Malcolm Knowles, especially in his *The Making of an Adult Educator* (1989), whose own curiosity propelled his insightful writings, shaping generations of future leaders.

Lessons Learned

Universities offer so much autonomy, even for administrators. Where else can you work as hard and long as you want, doing as much as you can, for adult education? For me, that includes developing a comprehensive understanding of our field and sharing it with others through teaching, research, and publication while consistently expanding opportunities for adult learning. The trick is to be efficient in your use of time and to move seamlessly from one activity to another. What personal goals do you wish to achieve that are unique to the campus academic environment? This is the least scripted of any other work setting I have known. Don't waste it.

CHAPTER 9

Quality in Continuing Education

Achieving Excellence

My thoughts about quality have undergone considerable change over the years in response to growing collegiate corporatism. The relentless pressure for universities and colleges, particularly in the public sector, to raise a greater proportion of their own budgets as an offset to decreased state allocations has forced a major shift in attitude throughout academia. In the not-too-distant past public colleges more closely resembled utilities with limited monopolies and could be guaranteed enrollments and the necessary operating funds for the services they provided. Higher education was seen as a form of public service, and the obligation of the state to educate its citizens was accepted as a given.

This set of assumptions is no longer in play. Instead students, the beneficiaries of higher education, are expected to pay a much higher price for this commodity, something closer to the real cost. Consultants are called in for guidance on how to position the university in the higher education marketplace in order to justify astronomic tuitions. Their advice could just as easily entail recommendations on what new majors to develop, or the creation of a college logo and "brand" so that the university can stand out from its competitors (Kirp, 2003).

Within this context, the quest for value takes on a different meaning and has more to do with perceived characteristics, as distinguished from measurable worth. The perception of excellence becomes *proof* of excellence. Former college debaters will recognize this as an example of the logical fallacy called *affirming the consequent from a premise*, without proving either.

Quality and its semantic cousin *excellence* are two of the most overused and imprecise words in higher education. The current accountability debate is an attempt to gain some clarity on what colleges actually accomplish as educating institutions. Outcome measures may be one way. Until we seriously accept the challenges of assessment and accountability we will continue to skirt around this core issue. In their absence, campus accreditation, through which a college or university is periodically evaluated by one of the six regional accrediting agencies, is the principal assessment/quality control process in the United States.

What typically happens is that every 10 years a team of evaluators, who are themselves college administrators, meets with a campus committee to discuss the institution's mission, its goals, and the issues to be addressed in the accreditation review. The campus then conducts a self-study focusing on these goals and issues. The completed report, after it is examined by the accrediting team in a follow-up visit, is filed with the accrediting agency. This report is never made public even though these analyses are able to shed more light on the meanings of collegiate quality than a score of *US News & World Report* rankings. It is a widely held belief that the demand for accountability will compel dissemination, in one form or another, of these collegiate self-studies.

Assessing quality at the departmental level is very similar to campus accreditation. A review team, composed of outside experts in the same academic area, reviews academic peers in another institution. Since at one time or another most senior faculty get to participate in the appraisal of their colleagues at other schools, it has become standard policy for reviewers to recommend greater investment by the university in the department, as a way of strengthening the discipline and promoting excellence.

Excellence in continuing education must be approached somewhat differently from that of the campus as a whole or from the academic department. The principal frame of reference for us is the *institution*, not the field or the accrediting agency. The dean or director establishes the priorities for continuing education in close collaboration with the provost, president, or other senior administrator to whom the head of continuing education reports. Excellence, from the institution's perspective, is determined to the extent that these negotiated goals are achieved. To speak of any other form of excellence, unless it is a means towards achieving institutionally determined goals, is to tread a short and hazardous path. Holding other notions of quality, such as those articulated by yourself or other professionals, is fine as long as they do not conflict with institutional goals. In an ideal world they will converge.

To achieve quality by both professional and institutional yardsticks is a noteworthy accomplishment and something we should all strive toward, even if our first order of business is to stay in business. Achieving excellence by the criteria of the university or college grants you the latitude to seek excellence by other, yet complementary, standards. In my case this amounts to innovative program development for the School of Profesional Development and my own professional growth.

Some may regard my definition of quality as too narrow or cynical. They might argue, perhaps like Leonard Freedman did in *Quality in Continuing Education* (1987) that quality is a complex construct made up of many factors, all important. There is quality in the classroom, quality in course appropriateness, quality in instruction, and so forth. Although this position is academically sound since it encourages us to think more analytically about our programs, it is of less value as a guide to job performance. Put another way, quality defined as an abstract, non-quantifiable measure of excellence is too elusive to be a yardstick of performance unless this is what the institution desires. And if that is the case, you are obliged to identify measures which can make the case for your school.

At one time revenue generation was not considered an important goal for my division. I paid minimal attention to

this standard. Instead I was expected to develop new programs and partnerships and was evaluated by those yardsticks. But in achieving the goals set for my school I also
improved the bottom line. Here is a different way of looking at it. Quality for the university is sometimes measured
by means of the SATs of entering freshmen; higher student·
scores imply better institutional quality. SPD offers degree
programs. What if, in a parallel manner, we raised the standards for admitting students to our degree and certificate
programs to improve our school's quality? And what if in
doing so, this reduced our enrollment and tuition revenue?
I think the response to this imaginary scenario would be
pretty obvious. A cash cow is judged by the quantity of milk.
Quality, as defined by student grade point averages, must
be within acceptable limits, but is purely secondary to generating revenue. The only mitigating factor I can see is that
as the finances for all of higher education become more precarious and unpredictable, all campus deans are being encouraged to generate revenue. Deans of continuing education are no longer alone. Although I am not happy with this
drift, since it goes against my notions of access and opportunity, this seems to be the reality, at least for the time being.

Teaching as Quality Control

My reasons for entering the SPD classroom were directly
related to improving my effectiveness as dean. It turned
out that the only students I was coming into contact with
on a regular basis were either those that had problems with
us or we with them. Usually it had to do with the unavail-
ability of a course, questioning the fairness of an instructor,
charges of academic dishonesty, or some form of unaccept-
able classroom behavior. While this was only a minuscule
percentage of the SPD student body, it nevertheless skewed
my perceptions since I was not regularly hearing from students who were enjoying our programs or who were without problems. I had also been curious to find out what it

was like to teach at Stony Brook in the evening...how the facilities were and that sort of thing.

Looking back, I can't remember if faculty were having problems with the physical plant. Their criticisms had more to do with the level of students and their fitness for graduate work, so this was also something which required first-hand information. On another purely personal level I questioned my own authenticity as leader of my school if I did not directly participate in its academics. In the academic culture of expertise I wanted to be accepted as an expert on continuing education not only in the larger sense, but also at my school, in order to better advance its goals and to refute inaccurate allegations by others. I did not seek any extra compensation since I was concerned that this might cause people to question my motives. So I began teaching regularly in the fall and spring, and even once in the summer session to see what that was like too. Later I taught online for much the same reason.

Teaching a course in SPD accomplished a number of objectives. First, I physically entered the world of the night school and began to see it through the eyes of both students and faculty. For example, I noticed lights on campus that were broken or poorly placed; you couldn't determine this during the daylight hours. I instituted a regular beginning-of-semester walkabout with the manager of the west campus physical plant. In addition to inadequate lighting, we focused on broken pavement, overgrown bushes— anything that we felt could possibly compromise the safety and well-being of evening students. I also worked with the campus concessionaire to upgrade the selection of food and beverages available at night, and with the college's audiovisual unit to simplify requesting and using equipment in the evening classroom. I can't honestly claim that I was responsible for major improvements. Yet I'm convinced that small steps in the right direction add up. One rarely, especially in continuing education, has either the resources or clout to effect major changes, so this strategy, besides being effective, is one of the few available to us.

From the faculty's perspective I experienced first-hand

the wide-mouthed yawns of tired (or bored?) students, late arrivals who were stuck in traffic on the Long Island Expressway (Distressway, as it is also called), sniffed the tantalizing aromas of food brought by students to class, and, of course, the imaginative excuses for late, misplaced, and poorly prepared assignments. I developed the skill and endurance essential to delivering a three-hour class and quickly learned that it is much, much easier to lecture than to engage students in discussion.

Teaching in my own program put me face to face with the reality of our clientele. I had heard that SPD students were poorly prepared and refused to work hard in class. There were also snide remarks made about their not being as smart as other majors on campus. I had to find out myself what my school's students were like. I discovered, much to my chagrin, a general low level of research and writing skills. As a result we created a seminar on research and writing to be taken by all of our matriculated students. The Project Seminar was to be taught by a specially identified and trained faculty, with the necessary motivation and experience to work with our students, who would all now be required to complete master's theses.

With respect to quality defined as a student's academic ability we had a complete range, from fair to excellent. Among our entry criteria was a 3.0 GPA, but you would be surprised and disappointed to discover that this was not always a reliable predictor of readiness, even if the student was a Stony Brook graduate. One of the consequences of adding the Project Seminar was that it helped students improve their research and writing skills, so the fair became good and the good, excellent. Also, the Project Seminar ensured that each student in the Master of Arts in Liberal Studies program experienced a graduate seminar and the chance to work closely with a faculty member. Even though our average class size was 22, faculty inclinations were often toward running these as small lecture classes. The Project Seminar, by contrast, had all the features of a graduate seminar—a smaller size (17 maximum), the expectation of full student participation, a tutorial-like relationship with the instructor, and time to conduct independent research.

Our only requirement was that students take Project Seminar before graduation. Although it would have been desirable to have them complete this course earlier in their studies, we never had the resources (and still do not) to offer enough sections at the front end. I was afraid that this could become a frustrating bottleneck and lead to many disappointments. So, although we encourage students to enroll as soon as possible, we leave it to them to make the actual determination of when. Not surprisingly a good number put it off until it is their final course. The silver lining is that many of them regret not taking it earlier, once they realize how much they gain from the experience.

Our evening graduate courses meet for three hours. Some begin at 4 p.m. and others as late as 7 p.m. In the beginning I noticed that my students seemed to be having a problem with punctuality, so the following term I scheduled my course to begin a half-hour later. Arriving on time continued to be an issue, so the following term, I pushed the starting time back yet again. Finally, it dawned on me that no matter when I chose to begin my course, some students would arrive up to a half hour after I began. The explanations were always plausible—a last minute problem at work, a highway tie-up, complications at home, and of course, trouble finding parking. Later, when we introduced online courses our school could offer the ultimate benefit to Long Island students: in-class parking, virtually speaking!

On another occasion I noticed that one student always arrived exactly one hour late. I discovered that she was taking another course the same evening, and it overlapped with mine. I asked her why she didn't leave the other one early instead. The question was left hanging in the air. Fortunately online courses now enable students to increase their course load without this type of juggling. And you can't fall asleep on the subway after class as I did while attending NYU.

One of the challenges of night school teaching is to engender lively class participation by students who are tired,

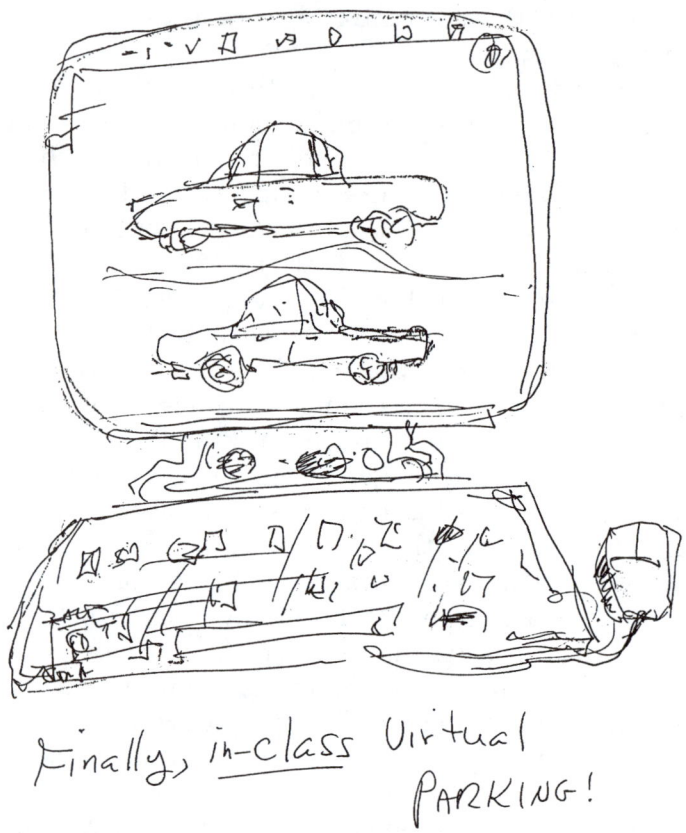

Finally, in-class Virtual PARKING!

hungry, or just stretched thin by their other responsibilities. I tried a number of techniques that appear in the literature such as group projects and presentations, rotating class leadership, provocative guest speakers who could spark debate, and just plain calling on people when nothing else seemed to work. The last technique was fraught with peril and potential embarrassment depending on how well the student had prepared. I learned never to take anything for granted, even with students who appeared to be involved. So, I found myself for the most part interacting with the handful of students who raised questions and who chose to actually join the class as opposed to passive attendance.

Backing off on my expectations could also be a problem since it was apparent that almost *every* student will conspire for a less demanding course. I suppose it is human nature to work only as hard as you have too except in circumstances where unusually strong motivation obtains. What happens is that some acceptable compromise is reached between teacher and student expectations. This is doubtlessly the thinking behind Knowles's "learning contracts" (1975). As dean I felt obligated to maintain high academic standards which to my mind meant plenty of assignments, especially written. In spite of this, my evaluations were very good. Students like enthusiastic, well-organized faculty who show them respect, even if the work level required is above average.

I also followed through on a suggestion made by Bob Boice, who headed the Teaching Performance Center, who recommended that faculty distribute to their students feedback sheets after the first three or four class sessions. I had these collected by student volunteers who would summarize and report at the following class meeting. The ensuing discussions were very worthwhile and promoted a better understanding of what the course was about and how student performance was to be evaluated. There were also suggestions about handouts, my talking too fast, and my illegible handwriting. I included in the feedback sheet some of the same items that would later appear on the university's end of class student evaluations. So I also deliberately worked to be a better teacher according to Stony Brook criteria. Overall the results were so good, especially in developing class cohesion that I began to do this in all of my courses. If you think about it, you realize that end of course evaluations, the point when these are customarily distributed, do not give the instructor a chance to improve that term. In contrast, by conducting your own informal one early on, you can fine tune your instruction immediately.

Another dividend in having students summarize and then report on their classmates' remarks is that it helps them to offer criticism in a positive way. I had to marvel at the sense of tact displayed. Since all responses were confidential, and I never saw them or even collected the forms, it would have been possible for these to be reported harshly.

This never happened. The recommendations made for my own improvement, and the way they were presented, served as models for our classroom interaction of mutual respect and commitment to learning.

I also taught in the summer session. This was not to my taste. I felt that there was too much compression, since a full semester was intended to be covered in six weeks. There was simply not enough time for students to reflect and do the careful, thoughtful work I required. I came to the inevitable conclusion that the same three-credit courses offered in regular semesters and then in the summer were *not* the same at all. Too much had to be pared away, and thus the course was not an adequate treatment of the material. But students expect summer courses and colleges see it as their obligation to offer them. A further motivation for the university is the extra revenue generated. Ironically summer sessions are a continuing education innovation designed for working professionals, especially teachers on vacation. Yet here I am arguing against it.

SPD schedules a generous array of courses but we always make clear that the summer is not intended to be construed as a complete semester in case students expect to take all of their classes that way. I don't believe that the summer session fairly represents the quality of our school, its faculty, or its programs. But for many of our students it constitutes a special opportunity when they are free from the pressures of work. The major problem is that it's not the equivalent. I compare summer session to traveling in steerage, the lowest category of accommodation on early 20th century ocean liners. It will get you there, but it's a voyage not at all comparable to what other passengers experience.

Teaching Online

SPD began offering online courses in the mid 1990s. After the first few semesters I felt I had to personally experience this too. There was, however, a unique feature of electronic education beyond curiosity that motivated me to get out of the starting gate quickly. Although all previous manifestations of educational technology never quite lived up to their expectations, my instinct told me that this time we had a genuine innovation on our hands. It seemed to be the right improvement for teaching at a distance, overcoming a number of the drawbacks of the night school, particularly the logistical, economic, and social difficulties associated with attending and teaching evening classes. I was sure, based upon what I had seen and read, that this would be the wave of the future, especially for part-time adult students and also for adjunct faculty. The combination of quality programs, easily delivered, a high level of student—teacher interaction, and the ability to select the right personal time for involvement in class activities would attract many new students and instructors to higher education.

I also wanted to implement this development quickly since I needed a compelling reason to leverage larger budgetary allocations for my school. I was very lucky that two phenomena converged at once, propelling us to action and ensuring dramatic growth of SPD's enrollment and budget. First was the nationwide enthusiasm for all things online. As more businesses began using email and the web for their transactions, and as home computers proliferated, electronic education became feasible. Although the first wave of virtual students stood out as technologically sophisticated, within a short period of time the ubiquity of computers and the simplification and standardization of software made e-learning the venue of choice for all distance learning, even among non-techies like me.

Despite these advantages, institutional resistance to teaching and learning in this new format would have been an insurmountable barrier for traditional colleges and universities were it not for the sudden visibility of the proprietary sector of American higher education which quickly seized a tactical advantage in this new competitive arena. At one point it seemed as if it was impossible to pick up a magazine, newspaper, or journal, especially the *Chronicle of Higher Education* or *Change Magazine,* without reading about the University of Phoenix or its brethren. I vividly recall one issue of *Educause Review* (March/April 2000) where Phoenix was depicted on the cover as a fire-breathing dragon laying waste to the higher education landscape. The *Chronicle* also added a special section on distance education in its online edition and one could count upon several items daily.

On my campus electronic education was a regular feature of our monthly deans' meeting with the provost. Except for SPD, no other school showed interest. I gave several presentations on Phoenix and on what I saw as the opportunities for Stony Brook. The additional knowledge I gained in preparing these talks, coupled with first-hand knowledge from my online teaching, added up to a strategic advantage which I continuously exploited. For five straight years I received additional budget allocations for online learning and expanded my base funding considerably. Even though our traditional face-to-face courses were oversubscribed I could not have generated the same excitement on their behalf. I concluded that there is nothing quite like a brand new and shiny bauble to get another senior administrator's attention.

Writing now, seven years later, we are still the only campus division with ongoing e-learning programs of any magnitude, and we keep growing. I suppose, from the perspective of the senior administration, our university has to display some activity in this sector, so we are a kind of distance learning "fig leaf" masking the indifference of everyone else. This suits me fine— less competition for scarce resources. Still, the reticence is surprising and at times disquieting. I wish others could look at it from the perspective of working students who are always short on time. They would then become distance learning advocates, if only for the humanitarian reasons of helping students juggle their adult roles as earners, parents, and community members.

The actual experience of teaching online was exhilarating. Doing something novel always excites me, and counteracts the additional work required of any new enterprise.

SPD's distance learning director gave me some pointers, and I then spent several weeks rethinking my course "Leadership in Complex Organizations" from an e-learning perspective. Although I had to modify it somewhat, the student outcomes were comparable to what transpired in my traditional seminars. I didn't see any difference in quality; quite the reverse, as students were able to improve their skills in writing and reasoning. The asynchronous mode gave them the opportunity to carefully think about their contributions, instead of just blurting out in real-time.

Quality is independent of instructional format. Rather, it resides in the degree of effort put forth by students and faculty in pursuit of learning goals.

Noncredit Programs

Not-for-credit programs have been the most labile area of our continuing education curriculum. I've heard that in community colleges, because of their long-standing commitment to vocationalism as a core activity, this is not so. But in universities, where noncredit is very much at the periphery, it has been tough going. Now bear in mind, prior to coming to Stony Brook all of my experience had been in noncredit so I anticipated a similar emphasis on Long Island. Yet I recall always having on my list of goals for the next year "put noncredit on a sound footing." This proved to be perennially elusive. First, there was too much competition from community colleges and the proprietary sector, the two major bastions for this activity. Second, the short-course/workshop was not the ideal teaching format for university faculty even if they appeared to have the necessary subject expertise. They had trouble identifying and reaching students whose needs were very precise and workplace focused. Thus, we came to rely upon consultants whose main occupation was training. But even with well-thought-out quality programs, the university did not automatically enjoy competitive advantage since the same consultants could be and were hired by other institutions.

Although it appears counterintuitive, businesses reduce employee training (and the hiring of new staff) during recessionary periods. They also slim down their human resource staffs. Prospective adult students, seeing this slowdown, decide that this is not the best time to take training classes since opportunities for advancement are limited. I've heard people argue that this is precisely the right time for adults to take training courses since there is more competition for scarce jobs, and additional training would give students an edge. Agreed, this is a logical argument, but not supported by behavior. Let me give as an example programs in Information Technology (IT). Following the collapse of the economy's high-tech sector and the September 11 tragedy, we were canceling IT classes right and left. And we were not alone; the same happened on campuses nationwide. Students would not invest in their education; they could not predict with confidence their success in a depressed job market. These programs also carried industry certification (Microsoft, Cisco, etc.), the highest hallmark of quality. It didn't make a difference.

Looking at noncredit, I'm forced to recognize the one critical liability that works against even the highest level of quality. This is the utter inability of colleges and universities, particularly in the public sector, to run themselves like businesses. Even universities which established for-profit continuing education training bureaus discovered to their disappointment and financial loss that it was still not the same; they could not quite operate with the agility or precision of the private sector. This is why colleges wisely subcontract the operation of their bookstores, food service units, and so forth.

This is doubly significant when there is no apparent difference in the product. Most training, except when it relies upon a special university-based expertise, is generic and easily commodified. Customers approach this in the same way as purchasing any other standard product, such as gasoline. Price and convenience are the determinants because we can be confident that 87 octane is the same among any of the major brands. Moreover, universities, public or private, cannot compete on price unless they are willing to regularly accept losses, or can convincingly demonstrate appreciably higher quality.

The exception, of course, is credit programs where public universities tend to enjoy competitive advantage.

Please do not get the impression that I wish higher education to be run more like a business. We benefit as a society from educating as many people as possible, and in the public sector this should be at the lowest possible cost. The major downside of uncritically applying the business/ corporate model to higher education is that students are seen as private consumers who, because they benefit as individuals from higher education, are expected to pay tuition at the level established by the marketplace. I fear that as tuitions rise to offset declining public support, a greater number of potential students will be priced out of a higher education. Or if they are able to attend through excessive part-time work and substantial borrowing, their education will be compromised. Yes, maybe this will mean more potential part-time students for continuing education degree programs. But unless the same variety, depth, and quality of programs are offered through our schools, the substitution of continuing education is second best, if I am honest about it.

Lessons Learned

The best way to look at quality is as a set of general guidelines appropriate to the role of continuing education within your institution. Put aside the hard-core academic values you were held to in graduate school. What are your "marching orders" as expressed by the provost and president? These goals should frame your activities, at least until you have more than met them. Then you can afford to have additional goals, as long as you do not neglect what you have been fundamentally hired to do. Basic continuing education goals, from an institutional perspective, usually involve achieving enrollment and revenue targets, or forms of outreach that put the college in a favorable light. Teach in your programs. It's the best way to find out about your school and its students. Determine where you have competitive advantage in the higher education marketplace and exploit these opportunities.

CHAPTER 10

The Futures of Continuing Education

Retrenchment and Administrative Restructuring

Directly addressing the topics of retrenchment and restructuring may strike you as a strange way to begin a chapter on continuing education's future. But since every year we hear about Universities X and Y which eliminated or radically reconfigured their continuing education units, I felt it important to take a look at this issue and then move on to more positive scenarios. Most deans and directors of continuing education live in apprehension of retrenchment, a danger that is always lurking, whether there is budgetary plenitude or scarcity. Under both economic conditions arguments are made to diminish or eliminate continuing education. When there is active demand for adult learning, separate schools of the university want to control their own programs in order to retain all revenue. And when budgets are bad, continuing education is frequently placed on the chopping block as something that can be given up with minimal negative consequences to the university.

I had to deal with a proposed retrenchment of my school about 10 years ago. The university's budget was being slashed by the state. Another dean, whose area incorporated all of Stony Brook's doctoral programs, and I received an e-mail inviting us to attend a meeting with the provost. I was on my third provost by this time, and something must have troubled me about this meeting, a premonition perhaps. I called my colleague and asked him if he had any idea why we were getting together, and he pled ignorance. A surprise

awaited me. At the meeting the provost and dean presented
me with their plan for subsuming the School of Professional
Development within the graduate school. There was to be
one dean having overall authority of graduate programs;
therefore my own retrenchment too! To entice me to accept
the plan they both asked what if I was to be the one remain-
ing dean. Of course I knew they were dissembling; they
would never put a continuing education dean over graduate studies at a doctoral research institution.

The lesson is the need for eternal vigilance when budget cuts are imminent. That is because no single characterization of continuing education structure and function is
normative. This definitional issue is one of the problems
we face when confronted by possible retrenchment or
reconfiguration of our units. So many variations exist, it is
impossible to argue that the current iteration at a particular campus is the right or only one. This is very different
from departments of English and History, which are obliged
to offer Shakespeare and the Civil War. On my campus the
summer session has been moved from continuing education,
to undergraduate studies, and until recently to enrollment
management. Now it is being outsourced to the individual
schools of the university, with no central coordination. Corporate training also has multiple homes depending on the
market segments identified and served. Most of SPD's activity is in part-time graduate programs, but these theoretically could be reabsorbed into the graduate school where
administration for them existed many years ago despite
great problems.

Thus retrenchment, at least in the eyes of those responsible for this action, can be clearly portrayed as a sensible
reorganization or realignment of an academic service. But
the reason offered, while entirely plausible, may not always
be the real one. In thinking about this subject, I've identified a number of factors that can help you determine if your
bureau is a likely candidate for retrenchment.

1. **Pushover**. Can the unit be eliminated without much
    of a fight or are there powerful allies who will come

to the rescue? Before you answer, think carefully. Are you out there by yourself without any advocates?

2. **Dispensable.** Is it the perception that the purposes of the bureau no longer make sense or are of questionable value so that there is no palpable cost to downsizing it? Or are you in the fortunate position as the sole provider of essential services?

3. **Competition for Resources.** There are never enough to go around. Are your resources, including the space you occupy, actively sought by other deans and directors? In a zero-sum calculation, would there be much more to go around if your unit was eliminated?

4. **Productivity.** A tough subject to discuss since very often "activity" in university life masquerades as an output. How much do you contribute to the college by your yardstick and by those of others who will make decisions on retrenchment?

5. **Fig Leaf.** Are you just an entry in the phone directory so that stray calls can have a place to be directed? "Yes, we have continuing education, call…." It only takes one person to answer the phone, so there is plenty of opportunity for downsizing if no real purpose is served.

6. **Settling Scores.** During budget crises someone, or some office, has to be offered up to propitiate the gods of austerity. And if you haven't bothered to make many friends, and in fact have been a very difficult person, this may be the time for others to get even. I know this sounds very juvenile, but it is a campus after all.

7. **Killing Many Birds with One Stone.** The elimination of a unit can solve many problems at once—a

demonstration of the ability to make "tough decisions" on the part of senior administration, eliminating a less productive marginal unit, redistributing scarce resources, in fact, any combination of the above. Sometimes a problem will remain unresolved for many years until the right circumstances for its resolution appear. I've seen this happen: a lot of griping about a poorly run office, but no one willing to tackle it, until a very tough budget finally made the decision inevitable.

8. **Ambiguity**. At one time I was tempted to see this as a weakness, now I'm not so sure that is the case. In fact, it may even be an asset. The caveat is, however, when asked "What does your unit do?" you must have a persuasive and comprehensive response at the tip of your tongue, not just the "Department of Everything Else." A variation of this question is "What do you do as dean?" If and when you hear this, even in jest, be aware that it is the proverbial tip of the iceberg and doubts about you and your unit are just below the surface.

Staying Viable

It would be easy for me to say "be productive, make allies, and so forth," but I'm not sure that stating the obvious would be of great value. From experience I've found that having good chemistry with your supervisor is critical. Mine have ranged from great to terrible. It's something you have no control over; you just have to accept. Yet even in the worst relationships, people (especially academics) try to stay objective. Otherwise the decision to terminate someone, or close an office, could be criticized as being made on the basis of personality, *especially* if there is demonstrated high performance. I'm sure this is what saved me from being shown the gate on at least two occasions.

The truth is that you never really know what is going on or how your unit is perceived. Therefore, you have to put the thought of retrenchment out of your mind and focus on the present and short-term future, say the next three to five years. Having plans is crucial for a long and productive career. I'm always trying to look around the next corner, trying to anticipate developments in our field. Even when you are certain about a good idea, it still takes several years to play out and prove itself. And you have to have other projects in the pipeline whether or not your ideas are successful. Especially if you are successful, since people will compare you against what you have already accomplished. Continuing education is one place where you can never rest on your laurels. The most successful programs have a way of going south, as in the case of Information Technology training.

I liken continuing education to crossing a river by stepping from one patch of ice to another. You've got to keep moving, staying aware of what is floating around you, focusing on your objectives. Most of all, you have to have the confidence that there will always be another patch of ice to step onto. There is nothing routine about continuing education, and for me that is its best quality. We always have new issues to consider, fresh initiatives to launch, contacts to make. Technology is evolving; the workplace is changing, always becoming more competitive.

A value-added aspect of continuing education is that many of its innovations migrate toward the core and become fixed in the culture of higher education. Summer session, distance education, programs with business and industry, cohort programs, and compressed formats are just a few of adult education's contributions. It's possible to see long-term implications in everything we do. For example, almost all colleges have Learning in Retirement (LIR) institutes for senior citizens. These campus-based programs have their roots in the Elderhostel movement which brought about a greater awareness of senior citizens as lifelong learners. The LIRs I know are primarily educational and social, not career oriented. But every day we read about the untapped labor pool of this rapidly growing cohort of aged 60 plus workers and retirees (Beatty & Visser, 2005; Dychtwald, Ericson & Morison, 2004). Is there some way for us to develop workplace training opportunities for this population as we have done for others?

Naturally, I am thinking of my own peer group as I too close in on my 60s. And, as I've said before (as in the instance of the Smithsonian course on Collecting Oriental Carpets), I can't be that much different from many others who want to stay in the workplace, but perhaps in other capacities and fields that we have not yet even considered. The information economy is favorable to us, downplaying the necessity of physical strength, offering flexibility and the ability to reach beyond our homes and immediate neighborhoods. Right now I don't know the answer. But I feel very confident that those of us in continuing education will play an important role in increasing options for this population. In fact, I recently attended a conference where I was pleased to see this subject addressed for the first time.

An Outsider in Academia?

The title for this section is borrowed from an article "Outsiders in Academe: Night School Students in American Fiction" authored by Von Pittman (1992). Although he writes about students, I am adapting his title to write about myself, and more broadly, about our field within the university. By and large we continuing education directors and deans must be largely categorized as people of action; why else would we be in administration? The appeal of having resources at our disposal, within the centrifugal, autonomous world of a college or university is a wonderful opportunity to do something of value. It may be to create and implement new programs or to develop procedures that simplify and improve life for part-time students, or in mentoring and advisement.

These capabilities should certainly place us at the core of the university value system. Why then do we feel so estranged? The central university activities of teaching and research, obtaining grants and writing books are not ordinarily ours. Thus we generally miss out on many of the attendant mundane rituals of campus life—grading, ordering books from the bookstore, serving as principal investigators on grants, having our own graduate students, which all combine to shape academic culture as we know it.

We address a population that is more transient than the average, a group that is also tangential to the campus experience by virtue of their hours or mode of study off-campus, weekend, or e-learning. We don't spend our days in front of students; we are usually facing computer screens. While faculty may be on campus for two to three days per week, we usually log 40 plus hours, Monday-Friday. We wear "office attire" and the faculty, well, you know how they dress. They have tenure and most of us do not. We think they get paid too much and don't do enough. They are convinced that there are too many of us and that we get paid for doing things of little worth which unnecessarily complicate their lives. They get off in the summer and on and on. Because we are responsible for all that takes place within our units including program development and evaluation, student and faculty recruitment, and often graduation, our world is one of mind-boggling complexity. In Italy the word *dean* is translated as *presidente*. This is actually closer to the truth in describing the range of our decision making and overall accountability.

Earlier I remarked upon the acronym CEO, Chief Executive Officer, and questioned its appropriateness for continuing education leaders. What about CEO as Chief *Education* Officer? I believe this highlights the most important responsibility we shoulder for our divisions and schools. We need to think of ourselves first as educators and only secondarily as administrative executives. Of course those skills are needed too, but unless we put education as our foremost duty, we will not be able to make common cause with the academic culture of the campus. I'm avoiding using the term *mainstream academic culture* in favor of Burton Clark's metaphor for academic life, "small worlds, different worlds" (1987).

It is both educationally and strategically wise to draw out and precipitate faculty interest in continuing education to create a campus subculture that is sympathetic to lifelong learning. As a source of ideas, resources, information, linkages with disciplines, and just plain support, friends among the faculty are essential. We are very fortunate that our work has its roots in campus academics. I meet a good number of campus managers whose lives are entirely within the realm of administration. They rarely encounter faculty unless there are problems. This recalls my own interaction with students until I began teaching. I wonder too, if continuing educators whose programs are noncredit have a more difficult time feeling that they are a part of the larger academic community?

Assembling a faculty advisory committee is one effective way of achieving integration with a broader swath of the campus culture. If you cannot readily think of anyone to serve on this group, this in itself indicates a problem. The committee should meet monthly; anything less frequent I've found to be a problem in maintaining interest and continuity. I would place squarely on the agenda the mission of continuing education on campus, especially its relationship to the faculty. A proposal and plan of action could easily arise out of these deliberations. I think the issue is too important to neglect and be left for others to address. As academic leaders we are obliged to enlist campus allies who will contribute their intellectual capital to our cause.

Often I find myself at meetings with other Stony Brook deans where very little of what is discussed is directly applicable to my school. Yet, not being there would be considerably worse. My ears are always open to things that might pertain to SPD such as an investment in e-books by the library, or a new academic major, or a possible budget cut. In all cases there are implications and opportunities for continuing education. Anytime I can observe my colleagues and learn how they tick is also useful in future dealings. And this goes for the provost as well. I try to maximize each opportunity for making connections; it might be a campus reception for new authors or the visit of a guest speaker. Doing these things is much easier when you are new and the need for ties is more palpable. But you can *never* afford to become isolated and cut off from the flow of information, no matter how long you have been on campus.

Jacuzzi Students

In a recent issue of *The New York Times* (Wintger, 2003) I read about the fierce competition for undergraduates and what colleges are doing to attract them including investing in multimillion dollar spa-like facilities featuring climbing walls, even Jacuzzis. I found the article baffling for several reasons. First, most of the undergraduates I know at Stony Brook (plus my son, Avi, who was a student at Plattsburgh State University, and his friends) have had at least one low-paying job. Some have two! If these kids, after working and studying, have time to spend much time in a campus recreation center I would be greatly surprised. These working undergraduate students, although younger than the part-time adults I serve at Stony Brook, are experiencing the same type of severe time compression common to older adults.

Let's look again at the "Jacuzzi students." They are middle class or of higher status. They can afford to shop around and compare colleges. If they are high-performing students, schools are actively competing to enroll them and are obliged to provide all the frills and options we have come to expect with any major purchase. Whether or not they are truly necessary we're convinced we need them. Anyone who has recently purchased a car has to be impressed with all of the extra amenities that now come standard. Of course the price of a car has doubled, but "look what's included." Well, the same has happened to college tuition. With these going up faster than the rate of inflation, 14% in 2003, colleges believe they must enhance the attractiveness of their package, especially to out-of-state students who pay a premium.

It is impossible, as we discussed earlier, for potential undergraduates and their parents to meaningfully compare the quality of instruction between institutions. It is far easier to count the number of exercycles, golf courses, climbing walls, food service options, etc. When my daughter Shari attended Goucher College I joked that every student received a pony since this small, private, formerly all-girls college maintains an equestrian program. I wasn't that far off the mark, the difference being that the students who went to Goucher in the early days could afford to bring their own ponies when the college positioned itself to attract the "pony set."

Parents and other taxpayers should ask if these frills written about in the *Times* are a wise use of scarce public education dollars. This question is especially valid when so many students need access to a low-cost public education. I don't think anyone could persuasively argue that these recreational frills are academically justified. When I read about the expensive Jacuzzis I think about the thousands of part-time students I have known who are desperately trying to get ahead. I think about the students at City Tech studying to be exterminators, welders, and hearing aid dispensers. The only frills they seek are an adequate number of courses at a reasonable (low) cost, frequently scheduled so that they can complete their certification program in as short a time as possible. This is also true for Stony Brook students.

We have gotten ourselves into a bind common to car manufacturers. In competing for the population able to pay the increasingly steeper tuitions, we are emphasizing non-essentials; the equivalent of cup holders, navigation electronics, and elaborate sound systems instead of reliable, trouble-free engineering. I am confident that most faculty would agree with me. They would say, put the money into hiring more teachers (and raising salaries too), improving laboratories, adding more computers, and increasing financial aid. These improvements will benefit all students, full and part-time.

Looking Back Toward a New Beginning

Throughout this book I've wrestled with the place of continuing education in higher education. The traditional academic hierarchies of research and traditional undergraduate/graduate teaching don't apply in any meaningful way to what we are about. Instead, continuing education exists outside of these parameters, occupying its own distinctive niche. This is a place where interesting and valuable projects are undertaken, and important goals achieved. It is a place for experimentation, for doing what others neglect or don't find important, and for fulfilling some of the most essential objectives of higher education.

The traditional hierarchies and their concomitant systems of valuation are out of place when we develop and deliver curricula for those underserved populations which are central to our operations. We stand separate, but parallel to mainstream activity, enjoying the benefits of collegial collaboration and the stimulation that is so much a part of the modern university. Among these, the exposure to new ideas and scholarly expertise are paramount. Being a part of this larger community of analysis and discovery should encourage us to think creatively and critically about our own programs, past, present, and future. This is one of the best reasons for participating in the world of continuing higher education— to imagine what might be possible, and then to achieve it.

I see other campus academic deans hemmed in by recalcitrant department chairs, who are in turn hammered by their faculty. I see provosts and presidents who are removed from the action and therefore compelled to operate vicariously through others to achieve their goals. Then I think of myself and my school and how we've been able to start and develop worthwhile programs, challenged by changing circumstances and opportunities.

Careers in Continuing Education

You can easily deduce from what I have written that ours is not a career for the faint of heart, the easily discouraged, or those lacking the ability to make plans and follow through. Being dean has given me a great deal of satisfaction, but only because I've somehow managed, with the help of a dedicated and creative staff, to persevere through the tough times when the frustration and difficulties were almost unbearable. This form of continuing education, in itself, has been priceless.

I've learned that what we accomplish is principally a matter of choice, personally and collectively, as members of a team. If the future of continuing education is bright it is only because we in the field continue to invest our energy and imagination toward making lifelong learning a reality. For somebody who just fell into this career by accident I certainly have a lot to be grateful for. But how do I feel about recommending this path to others, especially those just starting out? Knowles (1989) predicted 21st century opportunities for adult educator facilitators, technical specialists, and researchers (pp. 148-49). Judging by the spread of adult learning throughout higher education into most colleges, and also their internal divisions, he is on target. I know people in our field who have been responsible for continuing education in colleges of business, engineering, and pharmacy, even while the central university retained its own continuing education office. From this perspective I see many more options throughout higher education, even more than there were 20 years ago.

The mainstreaming of adult education in this manner, especially within smaller institutions, may make it possible for adult educators in those settings to move on to other key administrative positions in academic planning, finance, student affairs, institutional research, and so forth. This integration has many positive features since it is clear that the future of higher education in the United States will incorporate a greater sensitivity to older, part-time, nontraditional students who attend school in nonstandard formats, especially through distance learning.

Even if it is true that continuing education bureaus of the future will be smaller and more specialized, there will be many more of them, affording a profusion of career opportunities. And there is also the burgeoning proprietary sector which has staked its financial future on part-time students. What I have written from the viewpoint of a university dean will hopefully resonate with adult education professionals in all of those settings too. Our field will be numerically larger and also one of greater variety and vitality, if that is at all possible to conceive.

When I take the time to reflect on my own journey in continuing education I know I've made a difference in how thousands of people live their lives, not a trivial accomplishment at all. Should you choose to become part of this educational enterprise I'm happy to welcome you as a colleague. I wish you a career as least as exciting and unpredictable as mine. If you are the right kind of person you won't settle for anything less.

Some closing words of advice. Become involved in the professional organizations representing your area of practice. Access to colleagues is indispensable for success. Also the organization, through its activities, will keep you up to speed with the latest developments. Read widely and in great quantity. You always need fresh intellectual input. Teach and have contact with students. Give papers and write since it is only fitting that you share what you have learned with others. Despite what I said earlier about the institution determining criteria of excellence, learn the history of adult education so that you can place today's events and requirements within a more meaningful developmental context. In this way you will see that we have much in common with our former colleagues who faced and overcame similar obstacles.

Reading the above, I sound a little bit like Polonius in *Hamlet* (Act I, Sc. III) counseling his son Laertes who is embarking upon a long and dangerous journey. Polonius uses the phrase "neither a borrower nor a lender be" and other now famous homilies. In a similar vein, let me exhort you to set high and difficult goals that will take many years to accomplish. These will test your imagination and resourcefulness, and require you to enlist the help of others. More often than not, the outcomes will be problematic and you will wonder if you have actually succeeded. At this point it is good to recall your first years in continuing education and how far you have come. This should strengthen you to face tomorrow, and the days after with the same drive and determination.

REFERENCES

Armour, R. (1965). *Going around in academic circles:* A low view of higher education. New York: McGraw-Hill.

Aslanian, C. (2001). *Adult students today.* New York: College Board.

Bartlett, J. (1992). *Bartlett's familiar quotations.* (16th ed.). Boston: Little, Brown.

Bass, B. M. (1990). *Bass & Stogdill's handbook of leadership* (3rd ed.). New York: Free Press.

Beatty, P. T. & Visser, R. (2005). *Thriving on an aging workforce.* Malabar, FL: Krieger Publishing Co.

Bolman, L. & Deal, T. (1995). *Leading with soul.* San Francisco: Jossey-Bass.

Castiglione, B. (1959). *The book of the courtier.* New York: Anchor Books.

Chronicle of Higher Education (2004). *Median salaries of college administrators by type of institution, 2003-2004.* (http://chronicle.com/prm/weekly/v50/:28/28a02601.htm). Retrieved May 5, 2004.

Clark, B. (1980). *Adult education in transition.* New York: Arno Press.

Clark, B. (1987). *The academic life, small worlds, different worlds.* Princeton, N J: Carnegie Foundation for the Advancement of Teaching.

Clausewitz, C.V. (1989). *On war.* Princeton, NJ: Princeton University Press.

Cohen, M. & March, J. (1974). *Leadership and ambiguity.* (2nd ed.). Boston: Harvard Business School Press.

Conger, J. (1989). *The charismatic leader.* San Francisco: Jossey-Bass.

Cornford, F. (1969). *Microcosmographia academica, being a guide for the young academic politician.* (First published 1908). Arlington, VA: Beatty

DiCerto, J. (2002). *The saga of the pony express.* Missoula, MT: Mountain Press.

Donaldson, J. F. & Edelson, P. J. (2000). From functionalism to postmodernism in adult education leadership. In Wilson, A. & Hayes, E. (Eds.) *Handbook of adult and continuing education* (pp.191-207). San Francisco: Jossey-Bass.

Drucker, P. F. (1993). *Innovation and entrepreneurship.* (First published 1985). New York: HarperBusiness.

Dychtwald, K., Erickson, T. & Morison, B. (2004). It's time to retire retirement. *Harvard business review.* 82(3), 48-57.

Dyer, J. (1956). *Ivory towers in the marketplace.* New York: Bobbs-Merrill.

Edelson, P. J. (1976). Developing a continuing education alumni chapter. *Adult leadership,* 24(2), 260-261.

Edelson, P. J. (1989a, March 26). Reliving the simple joys of stickball. *The New York Times,* Long Island Section, p. 2.

Edelson, P. J. (1989b). "Transitions: Predicting the Success of New Directors of Continuing Education." Paper presented at NUCEA National Conference, Miami, FL, April 20-23, 1991. Available from ERIC, ED 336 542.

Edelson, P. J. (1991). Model building and strategic planning in continuing higher education. *New horizons in adult education, an electronic journal,* 5(2), 1425.<www.nova.edu/~aed/horizons/vol5n2> Retrieved April 26, 2004.

Edelson, P. J. (1992a). Assessing improvements in adult education instruction. *The journal of continuing higher education.* Winter, 1992, 22-24.

Edelson, P. J. (Ed.). (1992b). *Rethinking leadership in adult and continuing education.* (Ed.). No. 56 in New Directions for Adult and Continuing Education. San Francisco: Jossey-Bass.

Edelson, P. J. (1995). Historical and cultural perspectives on centralization/decentralization in continuing education. *Continuing higher education review.* 59(3), 143-156.

Edelson, P. J. (2000). *Weiterbildung in den USA.* Munchen und Mering: Rainer Hampp Verlag.

Edelson, P. J. & Ice, J. (2001). *Complete book of distance learning schools.* New York: Random House.

Edelson, P. J. & Malone, P. (Eds.). (1999). *Enhancing creativity in adult and continuing education.* No. 81 in New Directions for Adult and Continuing Education. San Francisco: Jossey-Bass.

Edelson, P. J., O'Brien, J. & Brennan, M. (1997). *Higher education's role in retraining displaced professionals.* Washington, DC: University Continuing Education Association [Monograph].

Freedman, L. (1987). *Quality in continuing education.* San Francisco: Jossey-Bass.

Galbraith, M. (Ed.) *Adult learning* methods. Malabar, FL: Krieger Publishing Co.

Gardner, H (1983). *Frames of mind.* New York: Basic Books.

Gardner, H. (1993). *Creating minds.* New York: Basic Books.

Ghoshal, S. & Bartlett, C. (1999). *The individualized corporation.* New York: HarperPerennial.

Gladwell, M (2005). *Blink.* New York: Little Brown

Goleman, G., Boyatzis, & McKee, A. (2002). *Primal leadership.* Cambridge, MA: Harvard Business School Press.

Gould, E. (2003). *The university in a corporate culture.* New Haven: Yale University Press.

Harvard Graduate School of Education. (1987) Fairhaven University, cases "A" & "B" (A5-87002A, A5-87002B). *Case studies in higher education.* Cambridge, MA: Harvard Graduate School of Education.

Heider, J. (1988). *The tao of leadership.* New York: Bantam Books.

Jones, L. (1995). *Jesus ceo.* New York: Hyperion.

Kett, J. F. (1994). *The pursuit of knowledge under difficulties.* Stanford, CA: Stanford University Press.

Kirp, D. (2003). *Shakespeare, Einstein, and the bottom line.* Cambridge, Mass: Harvard University Press.

Knowles, M. S. (1975). *Self-directed learning.* Englewood Cliffs, N.J: Cambridge Adult Education.

Knowles, M. S. (1977). *A history of the adult education movement in the United States* (Rev. ed.). Malabar, FL: Krieger Publishing Company.

Knowles, M.S. (1989). *The making of an adult educator.* San Francisco: Jossey-Bass.

Kunen, J. (1969). *The strawberry statement.* New York: Random House.

Lynton, E. A. & Elman, S. E. (1987). *New priorities for the university.* San Francisco: Jossey-Bass.

Maccoby, M. (1976). *The gamesman.* New York: Simon & Schuster.

Maccoby, M. (2003). *The productive narcissist.* New York: Broadway Books.

Machiavell, N. (1987). *The prince.* New York: Penguin Books.

Mintzberg, H. (1973). *The nature of managerial work.* New York: Harper & Row.

Morse, J. M. (1986). A little night teaching. *The American scholar,* 55(3), 403-405.

Pittman, V. (1992). Outsiders in academe: Night school students in American fiction. *Journal of continuing higher education.* 40(2), 8-13.

Roberts, W. (1987). *Leadership secrets of Attila the hun.* New York: Warner Books.

Rosenthal, J. (2004). *From the ground up: A study of the State University of New York at Stony Brook.* Port Jefferson, NY: 116 Press.

Runnion, N. (1969). *Up the ivy ladder: The delicate art of climbing in the academic world.* Garden City, NY: Doubleday.

Schatzki, M. (1981). *Negotiation, the art of getting what you want.* New York: Signet.

Simerly, R. & Prisk, D. (1992). Negotiating employment contracts for CEO's in continuing education. *Journal of continuing higher education.* 40(2), 14-25.

Skinner, D. (1999). *Introduction to decision analysis* (2nd ed.). Gainesville, FL: Probabilistic Publishing.

Stubblefield, H. & Keane, P. (1994). *Adult education in the American experience.* San Francisco: Jossey-Bass.

Sun Tzu. (1983). *The fine art of making war.* New York: Delacorte Press.

Wheatley, M. (1994). *Leadership and the new science.* San Francisco: Berrett-Koehler.

Wildavsky, A. (1984). *The nursing father: Moses as a political leader.* University, Ala: University of Alabama Press.

Wintger, G. (2003). Jacuzzi U.? A battle of perks to lure students. *The New York Times*, 5 October, 2003, pp. A1, 24.

INDEX